HOCUS POCUS

HOCUS POCUS

Walking by Sight not by Faith

JAMES Z. COX

But in the imaginary mind of humankind, there
are no gods to be found in all existence.

Charleston, SC
www.PalmettoPublishing.com

Hocus Pocus
Copyright © 2023 by James Z. Cox

Unless otherwise noted, all Scripture quotations are from
the Holy Bible, King James Version (KJV).

First Edition
Library of Congress Control Number: 2023912699

Hardcover ISBN: 979-8-9872968-1-3
Paperback ISBN: 979-8-9872968-2-0
eBook ISBN: 979-8-9872968-0-6

This book is dedicated to my beautiful, loving wife, Emelita, for in the garden of life, you are my favorite flower. Thank you for teaching me how to dance in the rain. I love you.

Contents

Preface

Since the infancy of civilization, humankind has asked the age-old question, How is it that we be? Or why do humanity and all creation exist? Over the ages the greatest of minds and not-so-great minds have attempted to answer these most profound and thought-provoking questions: How is it that humans, composed of matter and energy, exist within this space and time? Not only do human beings physically exist, like the tree, the butterfly, or the great fish of the oceans and seas, human beings are conscious of their existence.

Let's pause for a moment. What is consciousness? Consciousness is generally defined as awareness of one's body and one's environment. The tree is a living thing yet does not possess consciousness the way a human being does. Further, humankind possesses more than just consciousness; human beings are self-aware. It is generally stated that while consciousness is being aware of one's environment and body, self-awareness is the recognition of that awareness. Human beings are aware of the reality of being. Does the rodent possess self-awareness? Does the mighty lion? On a hot summer day while in between naps on the plains of the Serengeti, does the king of beasts ponder its existence? How did humankind physically come into this existence, and how is it that human beings have a level of awareness of being unlike that of the falcon in the sky?

We are physically here in existence and also possess, inside this matter that we call our bodies, chemicals that give rise to emotions and feelings. Think about that for a moment: it is incredible that we physically exist, yet still, within us, there exists that which one cannot measure, weigh on a scale, or extract to be placed under a microscope and visually observed—feelings and emotions. If human beings did not exist, no other living organism in the known cosmos would ponder its origins or the origins of time. No other living thing would come to know of its existence to the degree exemplified in beings called humans.

Humans are the only animals with the ability to examine, with the purpose of discovery and understanding, the mysteries of this extraordinary reality called life. Humankind is alone in this inquiry.

Again, I ask, How is it that we be, and why? All forms of life on this planet are astonishing, from the smallest living organisms to the largest creatures, like the great blue whale, all coexisting on this lone astronomical object known to harbor life, which man has named Earth. What is the genesis of it all? Humans are the only beings known that seek to understand their origins, self, environment, and everything that they can see, hear, touch, smell, and taste—and also those things that they cannot experience without greater exploration using the human senses. It could be stated with great confidence that no other life-form on planet Earth concerns itself with the origins of its kind or the genesis of time, yet humankind does—but why? How is it that the animal called humankind is designed to ask why? And if humankind is naturally designed to ask why, then is humankind, too, designed to uncover the mysteries to these puzzles of life? How is it that humankind possesses the desire and need to know the answers to these most profound questions?

Thus, if nature has placed the seed of curiosity within humankind, then it is possible that nature has also placed the seed of adequate intelligence within humankind so humankind can eventually uncover the answers to the questions sought.

Simply put, if humankind is incredibly biologically designed to ask why, then is this unique being essentially designed to ultimately know? For if humankind is not to know, then why has nature endowed the animal called humankind with the astonishing capability of desiring or needing to know?

The ability to ponder the origins of one's very own existence and that of all creation should not be taken for granted, for incredibly, no other forms of life on the planet possess this ability except for the animal called humankind, yet why? If we are endowed with the mental capacity to ask how we arrived here, then are we endowed, too, with the ability to someday answer the questions of the genesis of time and of humankind? What caused such an incredible existence to spring forth?

The universe, Earth, and human beings exist. We are here, but how did we arrive here? How are we to know? Again, I am compelled to ask, Are we designed with the capability to ultimately know? If humankind is not capable of ever knowing, then why is humankind biologically wired with the need to know? How is it that human beings exist within this thing called life—how impossible is it that this existence be possible?

The two front-runners that attempt to answer the questions of the origins of time and humanity are the big bang theory and the God theory. The big bang theory is a scientific theory. Wikipedia defines *scientific theory* as "an explanation of an aspect of the natural world that can be repeatedly tested and verified in accordance with the scientific method, using accepted protocols of observation, measurement, and evaluation of results." [1] If one were to subscribe to this theory that the big bang initiated everything, then surely one must ask, What caused the big bang to go, well, bang?

With the big bang, scientists think, the universe was born, and even as I write this sentence at this very moment, according to cosmologists, the universe is still expanding! Cosmologists state that ever since the cosmic explosion known as the big bang, the universe has

---

1   Wikipedia, "Scientific theory," January 11, 2023, https://en.wikipedia.org/wiki/Scientific_theory#:~:text=A%20scientific%20theory%20is%20a,accounts%20of%20the%20real%20world

been expanding outward, which prompts the questions, What is there in outer space before the universe encompasses it with space in its expansion? And is there a limit to the expansion of the universe? If so, once we reach that wall of limitation, will the universe contract and eventually destroy our universe, our galaxy, the planet, and the human race eons from now? And if there is not a wall of limitation to this expansion, is the stuff that the universe is expanding into infinite? If so, then how so?

Many cannot accept this *bang*-then-everything-was theory. After all, how could everything that exists, with all its complexities, have just come together so perfectly from a hot, dense bundle of energy in what is known as the big bang? How was it possible for such a complex web of existence to spring forth from a random cosmic explosion? Even a seemingly simple leaf on a tree has cellular complexity. I challenge the reader to put aside a few minutes to do a quick study of the anatomy and biology of a tree leaf. It is truly fascinating!

But at the end of the day, the big bang theory is simply that: a theory. It is possible that a big bang never happened. One alternative competing scientific theory is or was the theory of the steady-state universe. This type of universe would be infinite, with no beginning or end, unlike that described by the big bang theory, which is believed to have been birthed in fire and to be destined to die in ice trillions of years from now. The steady-state theory, like other scientific explanations other than the big bang theory, is now rejected by the vast majority of cosmologists, this rejection making the big bang theory the most accepted scientific theory in regard to explaining the origins of time and life.

The big bang theory was born of the observation that other galaxies are moving away from our galaxy at great speed in all directions, as if they had all been propelled by an explosive force. The big bang hypothesis states that the current and past matter in the universe came into existence at the same time, over thirteen billion years ago. At this time, all matter was compacted into a very small ball with infinite density and intense heat, called a singularity. A singularity is defined as a point of infinite density and infinitesimal volume at which space and time become infinitely distorted, according to the theory of general relativity.

According to the big bang theory, a gravitational singularity existed at the beginning of the universe. Something the size of a subatomic particle inflated to an unimaginably huge size in a fraction of a second, and the observable universe was born. Earlier I asked innocently, What caused the big bang to go bang? Stephen Hawking is quoted as saying, "Asking what came before the Big Bang…would be like asking what lies south of the South Pole." Stephen Hawking's idea that the universe had no beginning is enough to make your head pop! He is also quoted as saying, "There was never a Big Bang that produced something from nothing. It just seemed that way from mankind's point of perspective."

Still, if one is to subscribe to the big bang theory, one must ask, Where did the initial energy come from? One could argue that time couldn't have started with the big bang because something preceded it. Like others, I, too, hope that the big bang theory does not define the limit of how far the human mind can explore.

So then surely there must be a designer, right? So let us turn to the God theory. The God theory is faith based, or, in other words, belief without evidence, unlike the scientific theory of the big bang, which utilizes scientific explanation based on testing and verification. The God theory is based solely in faith.

Let us revisit the word *faith* so that we get a clear understanding of the definition. *Merriam-Webster* defines faith as "firm belief in something for which there is no proof." [2] Imagine that: believing something to be factual without facts or evidence. Is this logical or wise if we are attempting to truly understand how time and humanity began? Do we really want to conclude the investigation of the origins of time and of humankind on the basis of faith or religious beliefs?

---

2   Merriam-Webster, Faith Definition & Meaning, January 30, 2023, https://www.merriam-webster.com/dictionary/faith.

It is reasonable to conclude, however, that we have two options primarily. We can either seek out the answers to the origins of time and of humankind through scientific research—which would involve the collection, organization, and analysis of information to increase our understanding of the most profound questions humanity has ever asked—or simply believe on the basis of religion that once upon a time a male god who supposedly currently resides outside the cosmos popped out of nowhere because there was nothing and said, "Let there be something," and everything was.

Let's probe further on this. What if humanity had utilized religion instead of scientific research and discovery to develop the automobile, aircraft, medicines, lifesaving medical procedures, and other advanced modern-day technologies that we benefit from and enjoy today? Would we still have produced these magnificent inventions? When humans looked up into the sky and observed birds in flight, they wondered how it was possible for birds to fly and not human beings, and through scientific research, humankind invented the airplane. Does any reasonable man or woman today think humans would be able to traverse the skies as they do if humankind had simply left it to faith in a religion that one day humans would travel by air?

It is scientific research and discovery that has propelled humankind to a greater understanding of life's mysteries, be they those of physics, chemistry, microbiology, astronomy, mathematics, or one of the many other scientific disciplines. Yet religion, on the other hand, has never facilitated knowledge or discovery. Religious beliefs do not render discovery or move the needle of human advancement; they only pacify those who are content with simply believing.

What is so virtuous about having belief in something without evidence? What is so virtuous about simply believing in something for which there is no proof? Neil deGrasse Tyson once stated, "Science is a philosophy of discovery. Intelligent design is a philosophy of ignorance."

How time began and how humankind began are two of the most profound questions ever asked by humanity; therefore, it is not my goal here to be virtuous. The goal here is to derive a better understanding and uncover the answers to the greatest questions ever asked by the only beings in the entire known universe with the capability to ask the questions! After all, do we wish to uncover the mysteries of life through scientific discovery, research, and data analysis, or should humankind be content with answering these questions in a bag of religion and calling it a day? Religious beliefs have no place where truth determined by empirical evidence is needed. Which would one prefer when seeking knowledge: to faithfully believe or to factually know? Please take a moment and answer that question unto yourself.

So with the God theory, we encounter the many different religions of the world. A religion is defined as a system of faith or worship in a superhuman or in supreme beings who are immortal. A person that is religious or is of faith believes in a controlling power, such as a god, gods, or deities. Beliefs vary depending on the religion that is followed, and all religions past and present are beliefs based solely in faith. One must keep in mind that no one of any faith has ever seen the god that that faith claims exists. According to some estimates, there are over four thousand religions, with Christianity being the most practiced worldwide today. "Christians remained the largest religious group in the world in 2015, making up nearly a third (31 percent) of earth's 7.3 billion people, according to a new Pew Research Center demographic analysis." [3] According to this Pew Research Center survey, there were over two billion Christians around the world in 2015. Wikipedia lists the top four religions of the more than four thousand in the world in this order: Christianity, with nearly 2.4 billion followers; Islam, 1.907 billion; Hinduism, 1.161 billion; Buddhism, 506 million. [4]

Throughout the world, there are thousands of religions and within those religions perhaps millions of gods. How does one determine which to choose? It appears that when one considers the God theory,

---

3   Conrad Hackett, David McClendon, "Christians remain world's largest religious group, but they are declining in Europe," Pew Research Center, May 31, 2020, https://www.pewresearch.org/fact-tank/2017/04/05/christians-remain-worlds-largest-religious-group-but-they-are-declining-in-europe/.

4   Wikipedia, "List of religious populations," January 6, 2023, https://en.wikipedia.org/wiki/List_of_religious_populations

the first task is to select from the many religions that exist. This is truly a daunting task! What shall one use to determine which God concept is the correct one? For all the thousands of religions and millions of gods cannot be correct, correct? It is worth noting that in Hinduism, which is one of the world's oldest currently practiced religions, there are so many gods and goddesses that there is an ongoing debate within the Hindu community as to how many there actually are in the religion, with some believing there is only one god while some say there are thirty-three—and then there are those who say there are three hundred thirty million! An AP News article titled "Hinduism, with 330 Million Gods and Goddesses, Confuses Even Hindus," written by Dilip Ganguly, quotes a Hindu who said the following: "It is a way of life, where karmas (the results of deeds) are most important. Even to an average Hindu, the faith is so confusing." He added, "No one can explain how we got to acquire and where are our 330 million gods and goddesses." Ganguly writes, "Believers worship images and statues of gods and goddesses as well as live animals, including rats." [5]

The number of available religions and the gods to choose from within these religions is quite extensive, yet not one theist has ever seen any supernatural being—one described as a god or goddess—outside of the religious statues, images, or texts that make or represent the claims.

So many believers seek desperately to experience their gods, yet not one human being has ever seen God? I've never seen God. May I ask the reader—have you ever seen God? The global population is projected to reach eight billion near the end of 2022, yet no one living has ever seen or will see God, according to the Christian religion's holy book, called the Bible. The Bible verse that speaks to this conundrum is John 1:18, "No man hath seen God at any time; the only begotten Son, which is in the bosom of the Father, he hath declared him." This verse contradicts Exodus 33:11, "And the Lord spake unto Moses face to face, as a man speaketh unto his friend. And he turned again into

5   Dilip Ganguly, "Hinduism, with 330 Million Gods and Goddesses, Confuses Even Hindus," AP NEWS, January 31, 1989, https://apnews.com/article/24bfb9b360e30268ce87764b6f65bb72

the camp: but his servant Joshua, the son of Nun, a young man, departed not out of the tabernacle." Exodus 33:11 is then contradicted a few verses later, in Exodus 33:20, "And he said, Thou canst not see my face: for there shall no man see me, and live."

Here, within the same book and chapter of the inerrant and infallible Bible, Moses talks to God face to face, and then, soon following, God states that if Moses saw his face, he would die, for no man shall see his face and live. I do not wish to dive too deeply into this discrepancy at this time but feel compelled to say that if Moses was the only man to see God face to face, one must understand that in the secular world, Moses never existed, for there is no historicity of this Moses of the Bible. Further, if the God of the Bible were real and were truly all powerful, one might think that this all-powerful God could make it so that humankind could see his face without dying!

With the world's population currently nearing eight billion people and the majority having sight, still not one of us has spotted a god out and about. Nearly eight billion people, which makes for a lot of seeking eyes for there not to have been one human eye to witness this supernatural existence. This is suspicious, to say the least, with so many literally looking for God, yet not one living or previously living human having ever seen God outside claims made in religious texts. Why haven't the gods or God revealed himself or themselves to humanity?

Perhaps God is shy. I jest. But one must ask, Why would gods or God exist and never ever be seen, and if these gods or God created humankind with vision, why wouldn't God want to be seen visually by humanity? Eye-care experts state that after the brain, the eyes are the most complex organs of the human body, and they are described as having over two million moving parts, which can process thirty-six thousand bits of information every hour. Also, the medical world reports that 80 percent of what we learn is learned through our eyes. The purpose for pointing out these incredible medical facts regarding human eyes is to lead one to ask, Why would a god create humans with such extremely complex and sophisticated instruments for sight yet choose to stay out of the sight of humanity? It is interesting to note that the all-loving biblical God possesses flawed humanlike attributes; he is also self-described as a jealous god, as stated in Exodus 20:5 and also in Exodus 34:14, where the biblical deity states that he is such a jealous god that his name is Jealous! Exodus 34:14 reads, "For thou shalt worship no other god: for the Lord, whose name is Jealous, is a jealous God." The biblical God, who appears to perhaps battle with pathological jealousy and who desires and requires love, faith, belief, and constant praise and worship, would, too, desire to be visually seen in all his divinity, power, and glory by the human eye, for if this biblical deity were real and a psychological profile analysis could be performed on him, he would be diagnosed as a narcissist. A jealous, narcissistic god who requires excessive admiration, love, and worship would not hide from his subjects or choose to go unseen by humanity, for he would desire to be front and center in creation—a deity with a psychological profile such as this would desire to be seen and adored by all!

When taking into account how many modern-day humans (*Homo sapiens*) have ever lived, including the now-living population on earth, the Population Dynamics Research Centers have calculated that figure to be approximately 117 billion.[6] One hundred seventeen billion human beings, and yet not one human being has ever seen the biblical God—or any other god, for that matter—with the human eye. Christianity is the world's largest practiced religion in the world today, with a reported 2.19 billion believers, so perhaps we should turn to it for the answers about how the creation of this reality, man, and time began; after all, undoubtedly, 2.19 billion people couldn't be wrong, right? Outside the big bang theory, the God theory is the most popular option embraced by many throughout the world. Therefore, let us turn to the religion of Christianity for examination and particularly to its religious text, the book called the Bible, said to be the inspired word of the Christian God.

---

6   Toshiko Kaneda, Carl Haub, "How Many People Have Ever Lived on Earth?" Population Reference Bureau, November 15, 2022, https://www.prb.org/articles/how-many-people-have-ever-lived-on-earth/.

CHAPTER 1

Genesis

If we are to believe that the Bible is truly a divinely inspired gift from a deity, delivered to humankind through divine inspiration penned by human hands, a book containing written passages called holy scriptures, then it is our duty, as rational, logical, and intelligent beings who desire reasonableness, to investigate and analyze the claim's authenticity. In other words, the Bible must be scrutinized, thoroughly.

Ultimately the Bible is a book written by people—men, to be more specific, and I find it very interesting that there are no writings by a woman. All the Bible's books were purportedly written by men. There is, however, an intriguing theory that a woman named Priscilla wrote the book of Hebrews, for it does not mention the name of its author, but Hebrews is traditionally attributed to the apostle Paul. Then there is the Gospel of Mary, deemed a noncanonical text, discovered in 1896! Noncanonical and discovered in 1896? I find it troubling that the "inspired" word of God was still being dug up in the nineteenth century, even if the text is classified as a noncanonical text!

Scholars of early Christianity divide up writings into the categories *canonical* and *noncanonical*. I feel it safe and accurate to state that canonical texts could simply be defined as those texts deemed "inspired" writings from God and that noncanonical texts are deemed "not inspired." Who appointed and gave the early scholars of Christianity the authority to pick and choose which texts would stay and which would be omitted? Were they, too, "inspired" to select which texts were legitimate and reject those deemed blasphemous or foolish? Humankind's most profound questions have been asked since the beginning of time, and millions of people today believe that the Christian Bible answers all these questions and that the Bible is indisputable in its writings. This is truly a remarkable position held by Christians. So let us begin.

Genesis 1:1, "In the beginning God created the heaven and the earth." Genesis 1:2, "And the earth was without form, and void; and darkness was upon the face of the deep. And the Spirit of God moved upon the face of the waters." Genesis 1:3, "And God said, let there be light: and there was light." Genesis 1:4, "And God saw the light, that it was good: and God divided the light from the darkness." Genesis 1:5, "And God called the light Day, and the darkness he called Night. And the evening and the morning were the first day." Genesis 1:26, "And God said, let us make man in our image, after our likeness: and let them have dominion over the fish of the sea, and over the fowl of the air, and over the cattle, and over all the earth, and over every creeping thing that creepeth upon the earth." Genesis 1:27, "So God created man in his own image, in the image of God created he him; male and female created he them." Genesis 1:31, "And God saw everything that he had made, and, behold, it was very good. And the evening and the morning were the sixth day."

Genesis 2:1, "Thus the heavens and the earth were finished, and all the host of them." Genesis 2:2: "And on the seventh day God ended his work which he had made; and he rested on the seventh day from all his work which he had made." Genesis 2:3, "And God blessed the seventh day, and sanctified it: because that in it he had rested from all his work which God created and made."

I reference these scriptures because they describe the beginning of time and man, but before we address those claims, we must address "God rested." I'll be the first to admit that creating an entire universe from nothing has to be a daunting task, but still, God has unlimited power; he is able to do anything. God is omnipotent. Why would an almighty deity need rest when he is omnipotent and obviously had help? For it is written in Genesis 1:26, "Let us make man in our image, after our likeness." Believers of the faith will argue that God did not get tired and that God rested in the sense that he stopped creating, but it clearly states in Genesis 2:2 that on the seventh day God ended his work (stopped creating) which he had made, and (then) he rested on the seventh day from all his work that he had made. In other words, it is stated clearly that he ended his work and he rested. Therefore, if God's "inspired" word here did not mean "rest," then why is it written as "rest"? And if it's a misinterpretation by man and God is omniscient, why would God knowingly allow his word

to be misinterpreted? Or if God has unlimited power and is able to do anything, why did he not use this omnipotence to ensure his "inspired" word meant what he meant it to mean to all humanity without needing interpretation or leaving itself vulnerable to misinterpretation?

The word of a god would not put man in a situation of confusion and misinterpretation, for when man thirsts, he drinks water, not sand. Man never confuses sand for water, so if a god can fashion sand and water so man never confuses the two, why is his "inspired" word not fashioned as such? Whatever explanation defenders of the faith give for what the "inspired" word of God meant for the word "rest," or *shabbat*, which is Hebrew for Sabbath and comes from the Hebrew word for rest, it is still someone's interpretation, whether the interpretation is that it was for purposeful rest or that it served as an example to mankind that God did not desire mankind to be burdened with grievous work every day of his life. Simply put, if God's "rest" was due not to his being tired but to his being finished with his creative work or any of the other numerous explanations and interpretations that are voiced about the word "rest" in that verse, then the "inspired" word should have been delivered as such, for an omniscient god would have known that adding the word "rest" or *shabbat* would cause confusion. The word of God, I would like to think, would be comprehensible and not entrench humanity in bewilderment or confusion. After all, we are talking about the same omnipotent, omniscient, and omnipresent god that created everything in six days, perfectly.

Let's get back to the creation. God refers to himself in the plural in Genesis 1:26, "And God said, Let us make man in our image, after our likeness: and let them have dominion over the fish of the sea, and over the fowl of the air, and over the cattle, and over all the earth, and over every creeping thing that creepeth upon the earth." Now, I hope defenders of the faith aren't going to argue that the words *us* and *our* really didn't mean *us* and *our* in the plural sense! Again, we find ourselves decoding scriptures, attempting to understand who God was with when he was in the process of creating man and woman. For defenders of the faith, the most popular explanation here is that God is speaking as a Trinity, of Father, Son, and Holy Spirit; therefore, for the sake of argument for now, let's agree that yes, God was referring to himself in the plural. But if it is the case that God was referring to the Father, Son, and Holy Spirit, one should wonder why there is not a feminine representative existing in this Trinity: they invited in a spirit, but not a woman.

So we just read verses from the first book of the Bible, called Genesis, and its description of how all things came to be, but how can one be content with accepting these accounts as factual when these writings came from a faith-based religion? Christianity, like all faiths, is not contingent upon reason or empirical evidence. The book of Genesis is claimed to have been written by a fella named Moses who has zero historicity in secular history. Many Christians will challenge this lack-of-historicity argument with no evidence of historicity. If something is deemed true, it is based on facts, and we know that the Bible is a book of faith, but it still should possess an inkling of sanity. This book states that a god who is male and who actually has a name created the universe in six days. That's everything in it and outside it. Everything! It took this omnipotent god only six days to create every inch of reality, yet this same omnipotent male god took approximately

1,500 years to write a book—I mean, *inspire* a book. Think about how bewildering this is. The sun is perfectly designed; it was created in an instant by God. Recall Genesis 1:3, "And God said, Let there be light: and there was light." Those who read and know the scriptures should have a question here: they should ask, How could there be light on the first day of creation if the sun was not created until the fourth day? Regardless of which day it was said to have been created, the sun is by far the most important source of energy for life on earth, and the Bible states that it was created instantaneously. This ball of gas made up mostly of hydrogen and helium was produced in an instant! Yet this same God, who is male, enlisted over forty "inspired" writers—all men, no women, might I add—who took 1,500 years to create a text called the Holy Bible through "inspiration," said to be his word or message to humankind. Also, an average person is estimated to contain roughly thirty trillion human cells, according to recent research. If this god can create a whole man and a whole woman in one day, again, I simply find it incredibly puzzling that he couldn't have "inspired" a book in one day. I guess we could blame it on the inter-testamental period, also known as the four hundred years of silence, during which no one heard from the Christian God. This was the period between the writing of the last book of the Old Testament to the first writings of the New Testament. So for four hundred years God did not "inspire" any writings. Could one assume that God suffered from writer's block during this period? If God did not suffer from writer's block during this period, why, then, did God go silent for four hundred years? People were being born and dying, generations of people who would never receive this "inspired" word! From day one of creation, every generation of man has received the light and warmth of the sun. Was it not important for every generation of man to receive the "inspired" word of God as well?

Let's return to the said author of these writings, that fella named Moses! And who was this Moses fella? Again, it is worth noting, however, that what is factual about this Moses of the Bible is that outside of biblical scripture or religious texts, there is no evidence in the archaeological or historical record of Moses's existence. But how is this possible? Moses is regarded as the most important Jewish prophet! He's traditionally credited with writing the Torah and with leading the Israelites out of Egypt and across the Red Sea, yet no contemporary Egyptian sources mention Moses or the events of Exodus through Deuteronomy, nor has any archaeological evidence been discovered in Egypt or the Sinai wilderness to support the story in which he is the central figure. So, then, is the book of Genesis reliable, since there is no archaeological or historical data on Moses?

Let's return to the Holy Bible and see what we can gather or find out, at least about his burial site. So let's go to Deuteronomy 34:5–6, "So Moses the servant of the Lord died there in the land of Moab, according to the word of the Lord. And he buried him in a valley in the land of Moab, over against Bethpeor: but no man knoweth of his sepulchre unto this day." Well, how convenient…If that's not enough to make you raise an eyebrow. I guess only God knows where Moses is buried. After all, it could be and is interpreted here by many, if not most, that God himself buried Moses, yet there is no evidence that Moses existed outside the Bible.

As with the big bang theory, one should question the God of the Bible too. If God created everything, who created God? This is a legitimate question, and I'm aware that when this question is asked, we run into infinite regress, defined as an argument consisting of or implying an endless sequence of steps (e.g., when asked who or what created this god, one must then ask what or who created that god that created this god, and on and on and on the question goes: infinite regress). Regardless, what a commonsensical question. Who created God? I ask about the reality or creation of God because if there is no corroboration of Moses's existence in the historical records outside of the biblical text, then we have a serious problem, for if Moses of the Bible never existed, how could God himself bury a man that never lived? This impossibility would make Moses a fairy tale along with the biblical Christian God. Again, there is no evidence whatsoever for the existence of Moses or for any part of his life outside of the Bible archaeologically or historically! Moses, regarded as the most important prophet in Judaism, does not even have a headstone that one can visit or verify to this day, but how is this possible? The Bible states in Exodus 14:21, "And Moses stretched out his hand over the sea; and the Lord caused the sea to go back by a strong east wind all that night, and made the sea dry land, and the waters were divided." Wow, powerful stuff, isn't it? It is reported that the Red Sea's dimensions are as follows: its maximum width is 190 miles, its greatest depth 9,974 feet (3,040 meters), and its area approximately 174,000 square miles (450,000 square kilometers). [7] Therefore, how could a man (Moses) have been involved in an act of this magnitude, dividing a body of water on a scale such as this, and not one historian or writer of that era thought it was, at a minimum, noteworthy? Incredible! The historicity of said event, again, is summed up as follows by one of the top archaeologists of our modern time: "No archaeological, scholarly verified evidence has been found that confirms the crossing of the Red Sea ever took place." Zahi Hawass, an Egyptian archaeologist and formerly Egypt's minister of state for antiquities affairs, reflected scholarly consensus when he said of the Exodus story, which is the biblical account of the Israelites' flight from Egypt and subsequent forty years of wandering the desert in search of the Promised Land: "Really, it's a myth…Sometimes as archaeologists we have to say that never happened because there is no historical evidence."

It is believed that the pharaoh of Egypt during the time of Moses was Ramses II. Ramses is often regarded as the greatest, most celebrated, and most powerful pharaoh of the New Kingdom. We have archaeological and historical records of Ramses, and we even have the body! When Ramses died, he was buried in a tomb in the Valley of the Kings in modern-day Luxor in Egypt; his body was later moved to a royal cache, where it was discovered in 1881, and is now on display

---

7   Charlotte, B. Schreiber and Ryan, . William B.F.. "Red Sea." Encyclopedia Britannica, August 30, 2022. https://www.britannica.com/place/Red-Sea

in the Egyptian Museum! How could two people who lived during the same period and were archrivals, according to the Bible, accomplish great feats, but only one is heavily documented in secular history, while there is not a mention of the other? This fact should, at the minimum, make one rethink the historicity of Moses.

Moses is credited with the writings of the Pentateuch (five books of Moses)—Genesis, Exodus, Leviticus, Numbers, and Deuteronomy—yet there is no trace of his existence outside of biblical texts. Moses has no historical authenticity, and if it is true that Moses is a myth, then Moses did not receive the Ten Commandments from God and deliver them to the Jews under divine inspiration, and he did not author the Pentateuch! If Moses has no historicity and is therefore a myth, this fact threatens the authenticity of all the Abrahamic religions—that is, Judaism and Christianity and Islam! No contemporary Egyptian source mentions Moses's ten plagues of Egypt, from the first plague of turning water to blood to the last plague, in which every firstborn son in Egypt died, from the firstborn son of Pharaoh to the firstborn of the slave girl. Fascinating how Ramses, a historical figure, could have had such an antagonistic relationship with Moses and ultimately lose his very own firstborn son because of Moses, and yet there is nothing in the history books that documents this incredible story.

Let's thoroughly look at the ten plagues for a moment so that we can better understand why or how it was possible for contemporary historians not to record these events in the pages of history.

(1) Turning water to blood: Exodus 7:14–24

What's incredible here is that the pharaoh had magicians who apparently also could turn water into blood! In Exodus 7:22 it is written, "And the magicians of Egypt did so with their enchantments: and Pharaoh's heart was hardened, neither did he hearken unto them; as the Lord had said." In a simpler translation from the New International Reader's Version Bible (NIRV), Exodus 7:22: reads, "But the Egyptian magicians did the same things by doing their magic tricks. So Pharaoh became stubborn. He wouldn't listen to Moses and Aaron, just as the Lord had said."

Magicians capable of turning water into blood? Fascinating. Regardless, Ramses was obviously not impressed with Moses's messages from the god of the Hebrews or Moses's performance after Ramses's sorcerers miraculously performed the same act—to the point that Ramses left Moses outside and went into his house! Exodus 7:22 says, "And Pharaoh turned and went into his house, neither did he set his heart to this also."

(2) Frogs: Exodus 8–11

After that debacle, God apparently had to up his game and brought out the frogs! But yet again Pharaoh's magic men performed the same act, as stated in Exodus 8:7: "And the magicians did so with their enchantments, and brought up frogs upon the land of Egypt."

(3) Lice or gnats: Exodus 8:17–19

Here we have the magicians unable to bring forth lice, unlike God, and one would think God had won here, yet Pharaoh's heart was still hardened and refused to free God's people.

(4) Flies: Exodus 8:20–32

Pharaoh asked Moses to remove this plague and promised to grant the Israelites their freedom. However, after the plague was lifted, Pharaoh did not keep his promise. It should be noted that various sources use either "wild animals" or "flies" when describing the fourth plague.

(5) Pestilence of livestock: Exodus 9:1–7

So now God was surely growing angry with Ramses because God had already tried four times to get Pharaoh to free his people, so God decided to give all the livestock in Egypt an acute infectious viral disease, meaning the animals would experience fever and diarrhea and inflammation of mucous membranes. The grievous murrain was to be fatal, and fatal it was, for all the cattle of Egypt died! Verse 6 states, "And the Lord did that thing on the morrow, and all the cattle of Egypt died: but of the cattle of the children of Israel died not one." Still, Pharaoh was hardened, and he did not free the Israelites. It's incredible to surmise why no historian would have written something about this horrific incident: all the cattle in Egypt dead, yet nothing mentioned by the contemporary historians?

(6) Boils: Exodus 9:9

This verse now reads, "And it shall become small dust in all the land of Egypt, and shall be a boil breaking forth with blains upon man, and upon beast, throughout all the land of Egypt." But again, Pharaoh was not moved.

(7) Thunderstorm of hail and fire: Exodus 9:13–35

By now God had to be really mad at this bad man Ramses, and verse 18 states, "Behold, to morrow about this time I will cause it to rain a very grievous hail, such as hath not been in Egypt since the foundation thereof even until now." I guess at this juncture the pharaoh would have been amused by a threat of hail and thunderstorms. The pharaoh eventually got Moses to have God stop the rain, the hail, and the thunder, as he promised then he would let the children of Israel go, yet again, when he saw that the rain, hail, and thunder had ceased, the pharaoh did not let children of Israel go.

(8) Locusts: Exodus 10:1–20

For the eighth plague, God sent out locusts, and again the pharaoh said what he needed to say to get God to stop the plague. One should note that verse 20 states, "But the Lord hardened Pharaoh's heart, and he did not let the children of Israel go." God hardened the pharaoh's heart multiple times during the plagues, which means the pharaoh was not behaving of his own free will. Let us attempt to understand that. God wanted Pharaoh to set the Israelites free but made him powerless to do so.

(9) Darkness: Exodus 10:21–29

Verse 22 states, "And Moses stretched forth his hand toward heaven; and there was a thick darkness in all the land of Egypt three days." Imagine that three days of "thick darkness," and yet the historians are silent? I guess it is difficult writing in the dark. Verse 23 states, "They saw not one another, neither rose any from his place for three days: but all the children of Israel had light in their dwellings." How in the world could the children of Israel still have sunshine when there was "thick darkness" everywhere else in Egypt? And again, Pharaoh promised to let the slaves go after the darkness was lifted, only, yet again, to not keep his promise. But then again, did Pharaoh even have a choice? For verse 27 states, "But the Lord hardened Pharaoh's heart, and he would not let them go." Why would God being omnibenevolent harden Pharaoh's heart?

(10) Death of all firstborn Egyptian sons: Exodus 11:1–12:36

Verse 29 states, "And it came to pass, that at midnight the Lord smote all the firstborn in the land of Egypt, from the firstborn of Pharaoh that sat on his throne unto the firstborn of the captive that was in the dungeon; and all the firstborn of cattle." God made sure Pharaoh got the message this time, after nine attempts. God even killed the firstborn of cattle! Exodus 11:1 reads, "And the Lord said unto Moses, yet will I bring one plague more upon Pharaoh, and upon Egypt; afterwards he will let you go hence: when he shall let you go, he shall surely thrust you out hence altogether." Multiple times throughout the infliction of the plagues, the Christian God hardened Pharaoh's heart; therefore, Pharaoh could not have had true free will. The deity of the Bible was also confident his tenth plague would work, for he stated it as such, and of course he is omniscient, according to the scriptures. Could this omniscient god not have issued the tenth plague first to spare so much suffering and loss of human life and animal life? Apparently, as it is written in the scriptures, God interfered with Pharaoh's ability to free the Israelites of his own free will because God on multiple occasions hardened Pharaoh's heart! Exodus 12:29–31 reads, "And it came to pass, that at midnight the Lord smote all the firstborn in the land of Egypt, from the firstborn of Pharaoh that sat on his throne unto the first-born of the captive that was in the dungeon; and all the firstborn of cattle. And Pharaoh rose up in the night, he, and all his servants, and all the Egyptians; and there was a great cry in Egypt; for there was not a house where there was not one dead. And he called for Moses and Aaron by night, and said, Rise up, and get you forth from among my people, both ye and the children of Israel; and go, serve the Lord, as ye have said." The firstborn of all Egyptians were killed, and to make sure Pharaoh got the message, God exacted this punishment on cattle too!

Killing the firstborn of cattle caught my attention because God had already butchered all Egypt's cattle with the fifth plague in Exodus 9:6, "And the Lord did that thing on the morrow, and all the cattle of Egypt died: but of the cattle of the children of Israel died not one." How could God kill the firstborn of cattle when he had already killed them? Investigating the ten plagues of Egypt is an attempt to understand how historians during the time of Moses missed all this. It should be incomprehensible to the reasonable mind how there could have been extraordinary episodes of turning water to blood, frogs, lice, flies, locust invasions, the slaughter of horses and donkeys and camels and sheep and goats, total annihilation of all cattle in a country (Egypt), a thunderstorm of hail and fire, total darkness covering all Egypt for three days to the degree that no one could see anyone else or leave his place for those days, and the final act, the tenth plague, the death of every firstborn of Egypt—yet just as in the story of Moses's parting of the Red Sea, there is no record of the ten plagues of the Old Testament in any Egyptian historical records. Nothing on the slavery of the Israelites. Nothing at all. How can the Bible be the source to answer the most profound questions of man's existence when it can't even answer the question, Where is Moses buried?

Is There Proof outside the Bible That the Bible Was Divinely Inspired?
In our continuing attempt to closely examine the trustworthiness and reliability of the Bible, we must question its claimed divinity. How did the Bible come to be regarded as factually inspired by a god? Is there proof outside the Bible that the Bible was divinely inspired? Believers of the faith will most often point to 2 Timothy 3:16–17 which states, "All scripture is given by inspiration of God, and is profitable for doctrine, for reproof, for correction, for instruction in righteousness. That the man of God may be perfect, thoroughly furnished unto all good

works." But these are scriptures from the very book that is being questioned regarding its truthfulness; therefore, reading 2 Timothy 3:16 confirms nothing. What happened that verified the Christian Bible to be in fact regarded by Christians as the "inspired" word of God? What inspired their confidence in dismissing other ancient spiritual texts that predated the Bible and their god by thousands of years? Humankind is, believe it or not, an animal of logic and rationality; thus, reading something from a book making a claim is just that: a claim, not a fact, until it is proved to be factual. I believe any logical person would agree with this assumption.

Macmillan Dictionary defines reason as "the process of thinking about something in an intelligent sensible way in order to make a decision or form an opinion." [8] Recently, on December 26, 2019, *National Geographic* published an article by Rachael Bale, who wrote, regarding the number of animal species on earth, "A study in 2011 predicted there are some 8.7 million species on Earth, and we've identified maybe 1.6 million of them." [9] World Atlas states, as it pertains to insect species on earth, "Currently, over 925,000 species of insects have been identified." [10] So there are 8.7 million animal species and 925,000 insect species on planet Earth, yet humankind is the only animal capable of critical thinking and reasoning! The only animal on planet Earth gifted with the ability to think about something in a logical, sensible way. So again I ask, How does one know for certain that the Bible is an inspired writing by a supernatural, divine, and sacred deity? Is it reasonable, logical, or intellectually sound to accept the Bible as inspired by a god simply because the scripture of 2 Timothy 3:16 states it to be so? Personally, I fail to see the divinity or sanctity in a book written by men who claim to have been "inspired" by a god.

---

8   Macmillan Dictionary, "REASONING (noun) American English definition and synonyms: Macmillan Dictionary," January 19, 2023, https://www.macmillandictionary.com/us/dictionary/american/reasoning.

9   Rachael Bale, "How many species haven't we found yet?," National Geographic, May 03, 2021, https://www.nationalgeographic.com/newsletters/animals/article/how-many-species-have-not-found-december-26

10   Daniel M. Wambugu, "How Many Species Of Insects Are There?," WorldAtlas, November 27, 2018, https://www.worldatlas.com/articles/how-many-species-of-insects-are-there.html.

The Bible is a man-written production that took approximately 1,500 years to roll out to the public. A book that has been altered, edited, and revised by men; a book that has lost texts; a book that has added texts; a book where missing texts were still being discovered as late as the nineteenth century!

I could go on here, but I feel that the reader grasps the point. I fail to see the divinity in a book that is hailed as an inspired work of a god yet can be altered by man or go missing, only to be found hundreds or thousands of years later! It should strike one as incredibly suspicious that the god who was credited with being powerful enough to create the entire universe in six days and took a day off because he didn't need the seventh would need 1,500 years to "inspire" a book. The scripture 2 Timothy 3:16 surely cannot be the most compelling argument or proof that believers have for the "divine inspiration of the Bible" argument; after all, 2 Timothy 3:16 is within the Bible. Where is the proof outside the Bible that the Bible was divinely inspired? This is a reasonable question. What is the proof outside the Bible that the Bible was inspired by a god?

When this question is asked, believers of the faith point out scriptures inside the Bible. Believers' further using the Bible to prove that the Bible was divinely "inspired" makes atheists feel more secure in being atheists! Believers in the faith offer proof, pointing to their interpretations of the accuracy of the Bible, the unity of the scriptures, and the prophecies. This internal evidence of inspiration is ultimately subjective in nature. It relates to what the believers perceive in their faith in the book called the Bible.

Divine inspiration has been claimed by many religions for thousands of years; it is not unique to the Christian Bible. If the Bible were truly the inspired word of God, one ought to be able to expect it to have a clear and identifiable distinguishing quality or qualities that would be comprehensible by one's senses! Unfortunately, we do not have that distinguishing element or elements to point to, and this brings us back to the same question: What or where is this supernatural proof that the Bible is divinely inspired? And if believers of the faith cannot provide the needed proof, then all believers of the Christian faith have is an assertion or claim. And what, may I ask, is so divinely awe inspiring about that?

Fish cannot technically drown. Fish are physically incapable of drowning because they have gills and not lungs. If there isn't enough dissolved oxygen in the water they are inhabiting, this lack of oxygen causes suffocation, leading to death, but outside of this scenario, fish cannot drown, for they were designed with gills to live underwater. Birds are designed with wings; therefore, they are capable of flight. Imagine an eagle, if it were possible, deciding to walk everywhere it needed to go. One would question the health of this bird of prey. The spider is designed capable of producing silk that makes it capable of spinning webs, primarily to capture prey, but spider silk can be used for transportation, shelter, and courtship. Imagine if spiders decided not to use this unique ability to create silk. One would question why this insect would choose not to make use of its natural ability for its greater good, survival.

Humankind is the only animal on the planet designed with critical reasoning abilities. We are naturally wired to use them, and if a god decided to create only humans with this ability out of over 8.7 million other animals on the planet, wouldn't one think that a god would want humankind to use this stuff called reasoning? Please answer that question among yourselves. The incredible assertion is that the Bible is the inspired word of a god. The nonbeliever, reasoning, asks, "Says who?" The believer responds with, "Says the Bible." The nonbeliever, still utilizing reason, replies, "Who wrote the Bible?" The believer responds with, "It was written by man, yes, but under the direction or inspiration of God." The nonbeliever, still utilizing reason, quickly responds with, "Says who?" This question-and-answer scenario always ends with the answer being "man."

So should the world population accept the story stated in the Bible, in the book of Genesis, that the world was created in six days by a god? I googled the word *sane*, and according to Vocabulary.com, the definition is as follows: "a sane person doesn't have any screws loose—in other words, they're free of mental illness and in a reasonable state of mind." [11] The "reasonable state of mind" portion of the definition is the key part here that I want to bring attention to. Is it reasonable to believe in the creation story in Genesis starring the talking snake? Let us examine the validity of the scriptures in the Bible, such as 2 Timothy 3:16, for example.

The book of 2 Timothy is attributed to Paul the Apostle. Thirteen or fourteen of the twenty-seven books in the New Testament have traditionally been attributed to Paul, depending on which source you believe more. Let us run a background check on Paul the Apostle, often considered to be the most important person after Jesus in the history of Christianity. Hopefully we can do a better job with Paul than we were able to do with Moses. First, we need proof or historical evidence that the apostle Paul was a real person after sadly concluding, and reasonably so, that Moses didn't exist outside the Bible—though if anyone out there reading this has any verifiable evidence that can prove that Moses was indeed a real historical figure, please by all means bring forth that information!

What is the historical evidence that Paul the Apostle ever lived, or what historical evidence outside the Bible do we have to confirm that he was, in fact, a real, living historical figure? My research has gathered none. Outside the Bible, there is no historical record of the apostle Paul. Paul's purported accomplishments are that he made several missionary journeys throughout the Roman Empire, setting up churches, preaching the Gospel, and giving strength and encouragement to early Christians. Of the twenty-seven books in the New Testament, Paul is credited for writing nearly half, yet no historian of his time wrote of him. Christian scholars think Paul was born as Saul circa 5 BCE in Tarsus, in modern-day Turkey, and probably died in prison as a martyr circa 62–64 CE. Meanwhile secular scholars are silent.

---

11   Vocabulary.com, "Sane - Definition, Meaning & Synonyms," January 19, 2023, https://www.vocabulary.com/dictionary/sane.

Paul the Apostle is often considered to be the most important person after Jesus in the history of Christianity, yet there is no historicity. Aeschylus (c. 525–456 BCE) was considered the first great tragic poet; archaeological and historical records prove his existence. Anaximander of Miletus (c. 611–547 BCE) was a pupil of Thales and teacher of Anaximenes. He is credited with inventing the gnomon on the sundial and with drawing the first map of the world; archaeological and historical records prove his existence. Saint Augustine (November 13, 354–August 28, 430 CE) was an important figure in the history of Christianity. He wrote about topics like predestination and original sin. Archaeological and historical records prove his existence. And there is Confucius (551–479 BCE), who was a social philosopher. Archaeological and historical records prove his existence.

The very short list of historical figures mentioned lived hundreds of years before and hundreds of years after Paul. I've omitted popular well-documented emperors, pharaohs, kings, and conquerors. I've listed Confucius, a philosopher; Aeschylus, a poet; Anaximander of Miletus, an inventor; and Saint Augustine, a theologian and philosopher, among others. There is verifiable archaeological and historical proof of these historical figures. Paul the Apostle, the premier figure in the New Testament after Jesus Christ, has no secular historical record, yet Augustine of Hippo, also known as Saint Augustine, does? San Pietro in Ciel d'Oro (Italian for "Saint Peter's in the Golden Sky") is a Roman Catholic basilica of the Augustinians in Pavia, Italy. The church is the resting place for the remains of Saint Augustine of Hippo! Why don't we have something tangible as it relates to the most important apostle of the New Testament? Surely Paul's assignment in life was more important than the assignment of Saint Augustine of Hippo, if the Bible is to be believed as true!

The tales claimed of Paul the Apostle—persecution of Christians, conversion, prison release, the hunt for Paul described in Acts, the church planting—none of these events are noted by any historian of that time. One could argue that the stories of Paul are still possible, and that a man named Paul wrote half the New Testament; after all, the texts exist. The texts are tangible; thus, someone wrote them. But it is incredible to note that such an important man of the Bible has no historicity outside it. Again, Paul was "inspired" to write half the New Testament, so why didn't God "inspire" the historians of that time to write Paul the Apostle into the secular historical record, since it's apparent that the historians of that time weren't inspired or impressed enough to do so on their own?

As noted previously, I named just a few historical figures that lived hundreds of years before Paul and one that lived hundreds of years after him, and their historicities are well documented. Paul's mission in life, if one is to hold the Bible as true, had a far greater purpose, for he was divinely "inspired" by God to write half the New Testament, or new covenant, which is regarded as the new contract between God and Christians, thus bringing the word of God to the world, yet we have poets, philosophers, inventors, and theologians that made it onto the pages of history—but not Paul the Apostle!

The purpose of this book is to understand the origins of time and of man, not to prove Christianity an untruth, but millions of people believe that the book called the Bible answers all humanity's greatest questions. When I noted a few scriptures earlier, this was an attempt to explore the questions of the genesis of time and of humankind, yet using those scriptures for confirmation leaves one with more questions than answers.

The Bible appears to be a composite of historical and mythical people. How reasonable is it for one to be asked to believe in a person's existence when there is no evidence of that existence? The Bible appears to have factual discrepancies, yet it is viewed as the inspired word of God. But how can a book that is actually discrepant be a divinely inspired work of a deity, a deity that has created everything else in creation perfectly as it should be, without deficiencies?

Reasoning and critical thinking are among the most extraordinary of all the abilities bestowed upon any animal on the planet. Reasoning and critical thinking are two of the attributes that make humankind unique and set the humans apart from all other living beings. We are the only animals under the sun that possess these faculties. Humans are innately designed for reasoning, which is the process of thinking that evaluates a situation in a logical manner to come to a conclusion. Reasoning is genetically hardwired into the DNA of humankind. What reasonable conclusion could be drawn from not being able to find evidence of Paul the Apostle's existence outside the Bible? It's reasonable doubt. The revelation that we cannot find credible historical or archaeological evidence for Moses or Paul the Apostle begs the reasonable mind to further evaluate the credibility of the Bible. There is no historical record of Moses or Paul the Apostle outside the "inspired" writings of the Bible. Nothing. Moses, as stated earlier, is regarded as the most important Jewish prophet. He is credited with writing the Torah and with leading the Israelites out of Egypt and across the Red Sea. His writings gave birth to Judaism, Christianity, and Islam, yet there is not even a headstone marking his burial place.

Also, again, as previously stated, Paul is often considered to be the most important person after Jesus in the history of Christianity. Paul is credited with writing almost, if not fully, half the New Testament, but as with Moses, we have no historicity of him either. If these two authors never truly existed, what would this mean for the reliability of the Bible?

In our efforts to validate the Bible as a reliable source, as a tool to use in the attempt to understand the beginning of time and humankind, we must find the Bible to be dependable, for in the secular world we are governed by scientific facts and reason. In our examination of the "inspired" word of the Bible, we must find it as a reliable and trustworthy source. So if Moses and Paul the Apostle never existed and we have no factual evidence that they did, then we have a problem, for Moses and Paul the Apostle are said to have been prophets and inspired in their writings. Anyone else writing these Old and New Testament books accredited to them would not be recognized as having been inspired writers of said scriptures.

Therefore, since we cannot even confirm that two of the most important authors of the "inspired" writings of the Bible even existed, in the upcoming chapters of this book I will point out some examples of why I find it troubling to use the Bible as a reasonable option for answering humanity's most profound questions about the origins of time and of humankind.

CHAPTER 2

The Adam and Eve Story

According to the "inspired" scriptures of the Bible, a man named Adam and a woman named Eve were the very first humans the Christian deity created in a garden called Eden, thus ushering in the birth of humanity. Genesis 2:7 states, "And the Lord God formed man of the dust of the ground, and breathed into his nostrils the breath of life; and man became a living soul." And in Genesis 2:22, we read, "And the rib, which the Lord God had taken from man, made he a woman, and brought her unto the man." Unquestionably this claim would make Adam and Eve the most important people in the biblical texts and, if true, to all humanity. Yet again, one must ask the question, Did they really exist? Were they both historical persons or not? For if it is true that Adam and Eve were the very first human pair, that would mean that all humanity descended from that single pair.

But how is this incredible claim remotely possible, given the scientific data that contradicts it? One must understand that the Adam and Eve story provides the very foundation of the Christian faith, and should it be discovered to be an untruth, myth, or fictitious tale, then the entire religion of Christianity is false, and so are the other two Abrahamic religions, Judaism and Islam. Christianity's validity is dependent upon the Adam and Eve story proving to be true and not fictitious. In the last few decades, paleoanthropologists and archaeologists have been rewriting the story of the origins of humanity, not through an "inspired" supernatural force but through tangible fossils, artifacts, and other physical remains, thus creating major problems for the Adam and Eve story. For if we are to believe that Adam and Eve were factually the very first humans on earth, thus making all today's living modern humans their descendants, then, of course, we must conclude that Adam and Eve had to have been *Homo sapiens*, for this is the species to which all existing modern human beings belong today. Further, if the "inspired" word of God is claiming that two *Homo sapiens* were the very first humans on earth, then believers of the Bible have a major conundrum to make sense of.

Simply put, if modern humans were to factually be the descendants of Adam and Eve, that would mean that Adam and Eve belonged to the last group of human species called *Homo sapiens*, which arrived on earth last, and not first. When God was "inspiring" the prophet Moses during his writings about the origins of time and of humankind in the book of Genesis, how was it possible for God to omit the other humans that existed before and along with the two *Homo sapiens* named Adam and Eve? Since God was creating man in his image, why was there no inclusion or mention of the other human species, such as *Homo gautengensis*, *Homo habilis*, *Homo ergaster*, *Homo erectus*, *Homo rudolfensis*, *Homo antecessor*, *Homo cepranensis*, *Homo heidelbergensis*, *Homo rhodensiensis*, *Homo neanderthalensis*, *Homo sapiens idaltu*, *Homo floresiensis* (hobbit), *Denisova hominin* (Denisovan), or the Red Deer Cave people? The aforementioned were humans, not monkeys or apes—they were humans. Every primate belonging to the genus *Homo*, which is Latin for "man," is considered a human. I must also make mention of the genus *Australopithecus*, which is regarded as ancestral to the genus *Homo* and modern humans. These were bipedal primates with both apelike and human characteristics but were not recognized as human.

Man occupies a unique place in the biblical creation story, for it is written that man was created in God's image. This is the claim, and until the discovery of fossil remains of other human species that existed before *Homo sapiens* and alongside it, it was believed that Adam and Eve, along with their descendants, us, were initially the only humans to have ever walked the earth, for there is no mention biblically that there were other human beings in God's creation. One would not, or certainly should not, expect the Bible to mention every animal in all creation to prove that animal's existence biblically, but one would expect mention of other humans, for if man is the only creature that God made to be like him and to whom he gave rule over all other animals on earth, including every creeping thing that creeps on the earth, according to the book of Genesis, then surely the Christian deity would have mentioned the other humans. Also, if the Bible is claiming that God on day six created the first man in his image, then the first humans would not have been *Homo sapiens*, for this biblical claim contradicts the paleontological human fossil records and archaeological records of humans that walked the earth before the emergence of *Homo sapiens*, as well as the records of humans that coexisted and interbred with *Homo sapiens*. It is widely accepted among paleontologists and anthropologists that the first humans were *Homo habilis*, for this hominin is one of the earliest known humans and lived approximately 2.4 million to 1.4 million years ago in Eastern and Southern Africa.

It is also widely accepted that *Homo habilis* is the common ancestor of all later species in the genus *Homo*, including our own, *Homo sapiens*. Mitochondrial DNA evidence indicates that modern humankind, or *Homo sapiens*, originated in Africa about two hundred thousand to three hundred thousand years ago! Actually, one need not travel all the way back to *Homo habilis* to reveal the impossibility of the biblical *Homo sapiens* named Adam and Eve and the story of them being the first humans on earth, or to counter defenders of the faith who claim that all other members of the genus *Homo* were monkeys and apes or nonhumans.

First, let's understand what criteria literally make us human. Generally speaking, as stated earlier, a human is considered be any member of the genus *Homo*, especially a member of the species *Homo sapiens*. But what are the criteria for classification as a human being? "Paleoanthropologists have traditionally used one or more of four criteria to include hominins as members of *Homo*: an adult brain size of more than 600 cubic centimeters; limb, hand and foot proportions similar to modern humans; the ability to communicate through language; and the ability to manufacture stone tools." [12]

Let us now, for example, select two members from the genus *Homo*, investigate their distinguishing characteristics, and see for ourselves whether they meet the criteria for classification as human. *Homo erectus* and *Homo neanderthalensis* will be the selections. Let's begin with *Homo erectus*. The name literally means "upright man" in Latin. What did *Homo erectus* look like? An article in *Newsweek* titled "Meet the Homo Erectus: What Our Ancestors Ate, Looked Like, and More" says, "*Homo erectus* was the first of our ancestors to physically resemble modern humans. They were taller and their brain was larger than previous hominin species such as *Australopithecus sp.* or *Homo habilis*. They had a slightly different face to us: it was flatter with more prominent brow ridges. The long legs and the fact that they were fully upright meant *Homo erectus* individuals were efficient walkers and could cover larger ranges than their ancestors." [13]

How intelligent was *Homo erectus*? An article on the Human Journey website titled "*Homo Ergaster/Erectus*: Down from the Trees" states, "Living entirely on the ground and the first to venture out of Africa, *Homo ergaster/erectus* created the most successful tool ever invented by any hominid and may have been the first to live in bands of hunter gatherers and use fire to cook food…*H. erectus* were most likely the first to live in bands organized as hunter-gatherers, which would mean that they were able to coordinate their hunting behavior and most likely had some capacity for language. They cared for their injured relatives; and, as far back as 1.7 million years ago, created the

12   Mary C. Morton "Redefining Homo: Does our family tree need more branches?" August 16, 2016, https://www.earthmagazine.org/article/redefining-homo-does-our-family-tree-need-more-branches/.
13   Ian Moffat, "What the Homo Erectus Looked like, Ate, and More," Newsweek, February 02, 2019, https://www.newsweek.com/meet-homo-erectus-what-our-ancestors-ate-looked-and-more-1314344.

most successful tool ever invented by any hominid: the bifacial hand axe. Known as *Acheulean*, these stone tools are evidence of our longest-running industry, lasting well over a million years, with examples found from southern Africa to northern Europe and from western Europe to the Indian sub-continent." [14] (Note that *Homo ergaster* and *Homo erectus* are sometimes used interchangeably.)

Homo erectus showed up across the world after leaving Africa! This is a fact. Their fossils span the globe, and to be that successful in sea travel, surely, they must have had a way to communicate! There is an article titled "Did *Homo erectus* Speak?" that states the following:

> Evidence that *erectus* had language comes from their settlements, their art, their symbols, their sailing ability and their tools. *Erectus* settlements are found throughout most of the old world. And, most importantly for the idea that *erectus* had language, open oceans were not barriers to their travel.
>
> *Erectus* settlements show evidence of culture—values, knowledge structures and social structure. This evidence is important because all these elements enhance each other. Evidence from the *erectus* settlement studied at Gesher Benot Ya'aqov in Israel, for example, suggests not only that *erectus* controlled fire but that their settlements were planned. One area was used for plant-food processing, another for animal-material processing, and yet another for communal life. *Erectus*, incredibly, also made sea craft. Sea travel is the only way to explain the island settlements of Wallacea (Indonesia), Crete and, in the Arabian Sea, Socotra. None of these were accessible to *erectus* except by crossing open ocean, then and now. These island cultural sites demonstrate that *erectus* was capable of constructing seaworthy crafts capable of carrying 20 people or more. According to most archaeologists, 20 individuals would have been the minimum required to found the settlements discovered.

14   The Human Journey, "Homo Ergaster and Erectus: Down from the Trees." November 07, 2022, https://humanjourney.us/discovering-our-distant-ancestors-section/homo-erectus/.

Because the stone tools of *erectus* were simple and slow to evolve, some have rushed to conclude that they lacked intelligence for language. But stone-cutting implements are simply not the whole story. The evidence for *erectus* island settlements means that they built water-transport craft. *Erectus* seem to have had art as well, as exemplified in the 250,000-year-old Venus of Berekhat Ram. Further, archaeologists have discovered 400,000-year-old wooden thrusting and throwing spears in lower Saxony (called the "Schöningen spears"), which suggest a robust hunting culture. Thrusting spears, for example, require at least one member of a group to get close enough to the prey, such as mastodons, to pierce them with the weapon. Hunting culture entails cooperation and planning with others. [15]

Clearly, after reviewing their accomplishments in toolmaking, use of fire, sea travel, and art, as well as their outward physical appearance, we can conclude that *Homo erectus* meets the criteria for entry into the genus *Homo* and to be recognized as human. *Homo erectus* was not an unintelligent ape who swung from trees; they stood upright and was bipedal. It is noteworthy to add that fossil evidence for *Homo erectus* stretches over more than 1.5 million years, making *Homo erectus* by far the longest surviving of all our human relatives, for the current and last genus *Homo* member remaining in existence—that is, *Homo sapiens*—has only been around for approximately two hundred thousand or three hundred thousand years, depending on the source.

Let's now turn to perhaps the most famous of all the members of the genus *Homo*, *Homo neanderthalensis*, also known simply as the Neanderthal, who lived between approximately four hundred thousand and forty thousand years ago. Were members of this species human, and do they belong in the genus *Homo*, being classified as human beings?

Let's examine the Neanderthals as we have *Homo erectus*, utilizing the same criteria to see whether we are dealing with a hairy ape-man or

<hr>

15 Daniel Everett, " Did Homo erectus speak?," Aeon, February 28, 2018, https://aeon.co/essays/tools-and-voyages-suggest-that-homo-erectus-invented-language

another one of our human relatives. So what did the Neanderthals look like, and what other characteristics and attributes did they possess?

The word *neanderthalensis* is based on the location where the first major specimen was discovered in 1856—the Neander Valley in Germany. The German word for valley is *Tal*, although in the 1800s it was spelled *Thal*. *Homo neanderthalensis* therefore means "human from the Neander Valley." The Smithsonian Institution's website describes *Homo neanderthalensis* as follows:

> Neanderthals (the "th" pronounced as "t") are our closest extinct human relative. Some defining features of their skulls include the large middle part of the face, angled cheek bones, and a huge nose for humidifying and warming cold, dry air. Their bodies were shorter and stockier than ours, another adaptation to living in cold environments. But their brains were just as large as ours and often larger—proportional to their brawnier bodies. Neanderthals made and used a diverse set of sophisticated tools, controlled fire, lived in shelters, made and wore clothing, were skilled hunters of large animals and also ate plant foods, and occasionally made symbolic or ornamental objects. There is evidence that Neanderthals deliberately buried their dead and occasionally even marked their graves with offerings, such as flowers. No other primates, and no earlier human species, had ever practiced this sophisticated and symbolic behavior. [16]

After reading that brief summary of the Neanderthal, can we conclude that *Homo neanderthalensis* would have human rights protection under municipal and international laws today? For those who are still struggling with granting the Neanderthals the Human Being Membership Card, consider this eye-opening article by Donna Sarkar on the Discover website, titled "Could Neanderthals Talk? Breakthrough Study Suggests Our Ancient Cousins Had the Linguistic Capacity for Speech":

> Researchers at University of Binghamton in New York State and Universidad de Alcalá in Spain recently discovered that

---

16   The Smithsonian Institution's Human Origins Program, "Homo neanderthalensis," July 1, 2022, https://humanorigins.si.edu/evidence/human-fossils/species/homo-neanderthalensis

Neanderthals did indeed have similar auditory and speech capacities to modern-day humans. The conclusion was reached after various CT scans and 3D models of the ear structures of both Neanderthals and modern humans...The 1989 discovery of a Neanderthal hyoid, also known as the lingual bone, led to the suspicion that these species had the ability to speak. However, due to the different shape in their larynx than modern humans, this theory was dismissed. Now, the new study confirms that this bone was in fact used in a similar way to modern humans. In addition, they were also able to hear and produce sounds recognized today. [17]

In short, the Neanderthal had the capability to communicate by talking, and there is no reason to think that a species with the capability of talking didn't make use of it.

And for all those who still find it difficult to grant the Neanderthals their Human Being Membership, consider the fact that they had sex with *Homo sapiens*! And lots of it! According to an article written by Bridget Alex and titled "Could Neanderthals Speak? The Ongoing Debate Over Neanderthal Language," where the debate pertains to DNA, "The convincing aspect is that ancient genomes have shown Neanderthals and *Homo sapiens* interbred in several periods during the past 200,000 years. Realizing the groups were biologically and behaviorally similar enough to produce successful offspring has helped many anthropologists believe Neanderthals must have been capable of language." [18] The Smithsonian Institution report titled "What Does It Mean to Be Human" states the following:

Neanderthals are known to contribute up to 1–4% of the genomes of non-African modern humans, depending on what region of the world your ancestors come from, and modern

---

17 Donna Sarkar, "Could Neanderthals Talk? Breakthrough Study Suggests Our Ancient Cousins Had the Linguistic Capacity for Speech," Discover Magazine, March 25, 2021, https://www.discovermagazine.com/planet-earth/could-neanderthals-talk-breakthrough-study-suggests-our-ancient-cousins-had

18 Bridget Alex, "Could Neanderthals Speak? The Ongoing Debate Over Neanderthal Language," Discover Magazine, April 26, 2020, https://www.discovermagazine.com/planet-earth/could-neanderthals-speak-the-ongoing-debate-over-neanderthal-language

humans who lived about 40,000 years ago have been found to have up to 6–9% Neanderthal DNA (Fu et al., 2015). Because Neanderthals likely evolved outside of Africa (no Neanderthal fossils have been found in Africa to date) it was thought that there would be no trace of Neanderthal DNA in African modern humans. However, a study in 2020 demonstrated that there is Neanderthal DNA in all African *Homo sapiens* (Chen at el., 2020). This is a good indicator of how human migration out of Africa worked: that *Homo sapiens* did not leave Africa in one or more major dispersals, but that there was gene flow back and forth over time that brough Neanderthal DNA into Africa.

The evidence we have of Neanderthal–modern human interbreeding sheds light on the expansion of modern humans out of Africa. These new discoveries refute many previous hypotheses in which anatomically modern humans replaced archaic hominins, like Neanderthals, without any interbreeding. However, even with some interbreeding between modern humans and now-extinct hominins, most of our genome still derives from Africa.

For many years, the only evidence of human-Neanderthal hybridization existed within modern human genes. However, in 2016 researchers published a new set of Neanderthal DNA sequences from Altai Cave in Siberia, as well as from Spain and Croatia, that show evidence of human-Neanderthal interbreeding as far back as 100,000 years ago—farther back than many previous estimates of humans' migration out of Africa (Kuhlwilm et al., 2016). Their findings are the first to show human gene flow into the Neanderthal genome as opposed to Neanderthal DNA into the human genome. These data tells us that not only were human-Neanderthal interbreeding events more frequent than previously thought, but also that an early migration of humans did in fact leave Africa before the population that survived and gave rise to all contemporary non-African modern humans. [19]

Case closed; the evidence is irrefutable that the Neanderthal was just as human as modern-day humans! Dogs and cats cannot interbreed and produce fertile offspring. A cow and an owl cannot produce viable offspring. A man and a gorilla or chimpanzee cannot interbreed and produce viable offspring; they are not of the same species. Similar organisms can breed with one another and produce fertile offspring. This is because of the very different sets of instructions in each species' DNA. The genomes are simply too different to come together and make something that will live.

Generally, the genomes of different species cannot mix in any productive way to produce fertile offspring outside the uterus, the Neanderthal and *Homo sapiens* interbred successfully, and to this day, living humans carry the DNA of the now extinct Neanderthal! Regardless of one's belief or opinion, biological proof is the truth speaker here, in the form of DNA evidence. Many experts believe that the Neanderthal and *Homo sapiens* are two distinct species of humans. Other experts believe that there must be a reclassification of *Homo neanderthalensis* as *Homo sapiens neanderthalensis*, a subspecies of *Homo sapiens*. Afterall these two humans interbred and produced viable offspring!

Let's look at it this way: *Homo sapiens* and *Homo neanderthalensis* fall under the genus *Homo*, meaning "human," after meeting the scientific criteria and then being categorized, whereas the wolf and domestic dog, for example, fall under the genus *Canis*, which is the Latin word meaning "dog," after meeting scientific criteria and then being categorized. Now, wolves are *Canis lupus*, and domestic dogs are *Canis familiaris*. Both are closely related species of *Canis*, or dog. They can interbreed and produce viable, fertile offspring, very much the way *Homo sapiens* (modern man) and *Homo neanderthalensis* (the Neanderthal) did because the two are closely related species of *Homo*,

---

19   The Smithsonian Institution's Human Origins Program, "What Does It Mean to Be Human," September 29, 2022, https://humanorigins.si.edu/evidence/genetics/ancient-dna-and-neanderthals

or human! In other words, why wouldn't Neanderthals and *Homo sapiens* be able to interbreed when they both are human? This is essentially the same question as why the wolf wouldn't be able to interbreed with the domestic dog when they both are dogs.

Ernst Walter Mayr, one of the twentieth century's leading evolutionary biologists, once wrote, "If two organisms can breed and produce fertile offspring, it means that they belong to the same species." Today others are taking it one step further by suggesting that perhaps the Neanderthal and *Homo sapiens* not only could have been closely related species but also became one species in the end! A 2020 article by Josie Glausiusz, a science journalist based in Israel, titled "Were Neanderthals More Than Cousins to *Homo sapiens*?" states the following:

> New studies, made possible in part by computational techniques that enable researchers to analyze huge quantities of genetic data, show that *H. sapiens* and Neanderthals interbred far more than previously imagined. Indeed, their proclivity for pairing off has led many researchers to question the old dictum that Neanderthals and *H. sapiens* were separate species. Such ideas raise questions as to what it really means to be a distinct "species." They also raise the possibility that perhaps *H. sapiens* did not outcompete Neanderthals into extinction, as some scientists have suggested. Rather, one species may have simply absorbed the other—and so, Neanderthals, in a sense, could survive in us. [20]

The evidence is overwhelming that the Neanderthals were, without a doubt, human. The Neanderthal is credited with some cave art and currently holds the title for creating perhaps the very first musical instrument, the Divje Babe "flute"! The flute was discovered in the cave of Divje Babe in Slovenia and is thought to date back at least forty-three thousand to sixty thousand years, depending on the reporting source, its age making it the oldest known musical instrument in the world!

---

20   Josie Glausiusz, "Were Neanderthals More Than Cousins to Homo Sapiens?," SAPIENS, August 12, 2022, https://www.sapiens.org/biology/hominin-species-neanderthals/.

Its present location is the National Museum of Slovenia, Ljubljana. The Neanderthal was an artist and musician by these accounts, which demonstrate that Neanderthals definitely had the capacity for symbolic behavior and were imaginative and capable of artistic expression. The Neanderthal was a human being, and if they were alive today, after showering, getting a shave, and then being placed in a suit and tie, they could move throughout any society in the world without alarming the general public to call its local zoo officials!

Further, if that same Neanderthal decided to go to the local hospital where you and your family currently receive medical care, Mr. Neanderthal could donate blood! Yes, donate blood, because Neanderthals had type O blood. Well, what significance is that, you ask? People with type O blood are called universal donors because their donated red blood cells have no A, B, or Rh antigens and can therefore be safely given to people of any blood group. A recent study showed that Neanderthals also carried other blood types found in the ABO blood group system. *Encyclopedia Britannica* defines the ABO blood group system as "the classification of human blood based on the inherited properties of red blood cells (erythrocytes) as determined by the presence or absence of the antigens A and B, which are carried on the surface of the red cells. Persons may thus have type A, type B, type O, or type AB blood." [21]

The Neanderthals were human beings. And if the Neanderthals were alive today, in 2023, they would surely be entitled to human rights protections under municipal and international law. There is a fascinating article titled "What Does It Mean to Have Neanderthal or Denisovan DNA?" which reads, in part, as follows:

> Several direct-to-consumer genetic testing companies report how much DNA a person has inherited from prehistoric humans, such as Neanderthals and Denisovans. This information is generally reported as a percentage that suggests how much DNA an individual has inherited from these ancestors.

---

21   Britannica, T. Editors of Encyclopaedia. "ABO blood group system." Encyclopedia Britannica, May 22, 2020. https://www.britannica.com/science/ABO-blood-group-system

The percentage of Neanderthal DNA in modern humans is zero or close to zero in people from African populations, and is about 1 to 2 percent in people of European or Asian background. The percentage of Denisovan DNA is highest in the Melanesian population (4 to 6 percent), lower in other Southeast Asian and Pacific Islander populations, and very low or undetectable elsewhere in the world. Neanderthals were very early (archaic) humans who lived in Europe and Western Asia from about 400,000 years ago until they became extinct about 40,000 years ago. Denisovans are another population of early humans who lived in Asia and were distantly related to Neanderthals. (Much less is known about the Denisovans because scientists have uncovered fewer fossils of these ancient people.) The precise way that modern humans, Neanderthals, and Denisovans are related is still under study. However, research has shown that modern humans overlapped with Neanderthal and Denisovan populations for a period, and that they had children together (interbred). As a result, many people living today have a small amount of genetic material from these distant ancestors.

Scientists have sequenced Neanderthal and Denisovan genomes from fossils discovered in Europe and Asia. This genetic information is helping researchers learn more about these early humans. Determining which areas of the genome are shared with archaic humans, and which areas are different, will also help researchers find out what differentiates modern humans from our closest extinct relatives. In addition to the percentage of Neanderthal or Denisovan DNA, direct-to-consumer testing reports may include information about a few genetic variants inherited from these ancestors that influence specific traits. Studies have suggested that certain genetic variations inherited from archaic humans may play roles in hair texture, height, sensitivity of the sense of smell, immune responses, adaptations to high altitude, and other characteristics in modern humans. These variations may also influence the risk of developing certain diseases. However, the significance of Neanderthal or Denisovan genetic variants on disease risk is still an area of active study, and most direct-to-consumer test results currently do not include them. [22]

It has been confirmed through scientific DNA evidence that the Neanderthal and *Homo sapiens* interbred. Both *Homo sapiens* and Neanderthals also interbred with the Denisovans, which is confirmation that they (Denisovans) were human beings too! As we've already discussed, only like species can interbreed and bring forth viable offspring. These three members of the genus *Homo* had sexual relations and produced offspring successfully because these humans inhabited the earth simultaneously. I feel it safe to assume that at any time during the history of mankind, whenever there was opportunity for sexual encounters, the members of the different human species engaged in sexual relationships, whether forced or consensual, and interbreeding happened among the different species of humans—and it happened a lot.

What is extraordinary is that fossil history reveals that every few hundred thousand years, a new human species enters the arena of life. We are currently the last species standing, but will *Homo sapiens* be the last species ever to walk the earth?

Let's return to the claimed original man and woman, according to the Holy Bible. If Adam came from dust and Eve came from the rib of Adam, they entered the world supernaturally and also were fully formed, might I add—fully formed, meaning fully developed, and not as newborns. Keep in mind that the Bible is stating that Adam and Eve were the very first humans.

Let's take a look at Adam and Eve's biblical family tree, for their genealogy must reveal that they were of a human species other than *Homo*

22   MedlinePlus, "What does it mean to have Neanderthal or Denisovan DNA?," June 23, 2022, https://medlineplus.gov/genetics/understanding/dtcgenetictesting/neanderthaldna/

sapiens. We can determine which species of the *Homo* genus Adam and Eve belonged to by examining their offspring in reverse order.

Let's begin. According to the Bible, Adam and Eve actually had more than two sons, contrary to what is believed by many. Their named sons in the Bible were Cain, Abel, and Seth. It was from Seth's lineage that Noah was begotten. I am sure that the reader knows who Noah is, but for those who are unfamiliar with the biblical great, let me briefly educate you on the importance of the character named Noah in the Bible.

Noah was the man who, under God's direction, built an ark in which he and his sons and their wives and all living creatures would be saved from the flood that God was getting ready to dispatch onto the world because God saw the world had grown evil and he wanted to cleanse it. The biblical text in Genesis 7:4 reads, "For yet seven days, and I will cause it to rain upon the earth forty days and forty nights; and every living substance that I have made will I destroy from off the face of the earth."

After the flood the only people on the planet now alive were Noah's family. Noah had three sons, Shem, Ham, and Japheth which would make everyone alive today a descendant of one of the three sons, if the story were a factual historical event. Also, there is no mention in the Bible of Noah producing more children.

Here's the million-dollar question: Were any of Noah's three sons members of *Homo habilis*? I would think not, since all humans inhabiting the planet currently are members of *Homo sapiens*. And since the fact is that all living humans currently are *Homo sapiens*, that would mean that Shem, Ham, and Japheth had to have been *Homo sapiens*, too, if we are to be their direct descendants. Further, if Shem, Ham, and Japheth were *Homo sapiens*, this would mean that Noah was a member of *Homo sapiens*. Noah was a direct descendant of Seth, which would make Seth a member of *Homo sapiens*.

Now, remember, Seth is one of the sons of Adam and Eve, and therefore Seth's being a member of *Homo sapiens* would make Adam and Eve members of *Homo sapiens*! This would clearly mean that the story of Adam and Eve being the first humans on earth is untrue. *Homo sapiens* have been on earth approximately two hundred to three hundred thousand years; we are the last human species to evolve and not the first. This is a scientific fact.

Millions of Christians today believe that the creation story of the beginning of the world and of Adam and Eve in the book of Genesis is the literal truth about how the world came into being. According to these Christians, the universe and everything in it were created by God in six days, with a time span that biblical scholars have calculated to be under six thousand years ago. Human evolution is a gradual process of change, requiring hundreds of thousands of years to millions of years to produce changes in physical or behavioral traits. Therefore, if biblical experts are using calculations based on the chronology given in the Bible and their calculations' result places the creation of the world and the beginning of humanity less than six thousand years ago, this timeline would place the biblical Adam and Eve into the last group remaining of the human species *Homo sapiens* because of the time period for existing *Homo* genus members that did not go extinct.

In other words, if we are to use the under-six-thousand-years time frame for the creation of the world and of humankind, that would mean that whichever human species was in the Garden of Eden would have to be the same human species that found refuge on Noah's ark, and this in turn would ultimately mean that those humans' descendants would have to be members of *Homo sapiens*, which is actually what the world is populated with today. The problem with this outcome is that it contradicts the fact that our species, *Homo sapiens*, was the last human species to enter onto the world stage—not the first. The Adam and Eve story contradicts the human fossil record and science. This contradiction would leave one only to conclude, and reasonably so, that the Adam and Eve story is fictitious.

CHAPTER 3

Anno Mundi
Monday, October 7, 3761 BCE

October 7, 3761 BCE, is the date the world was created—according to the Jewish calendar. The *Encyclopedia Britannica* defines *anno mundi* (Latin for "in the year of the world") as "the year dating from the year of creation in Jewish chronology, based on rabbinic calculations. Since the ninth century CE, various dates between 3762 and 3758 BCE have been advanced by Jewish scholars as the time of creation, but the exact date of Oct. 7, 3761 BCE, is now generally accepted in Judaism." [23]

To determine what year is it anno mundi, one would need only to calculate by adding 3761 to the current year. This would mean that during this year of 2023, we will be in the year of 5784 anno mundi. This biblical calculation would put the age of creation at 5784 years old. The beautiful Hollywood actress Betty White has socks that are older than that!

So according to this calculation, one could imagine the Christian deity getting out of bed on a Monday morning when it was still dark out on the seventh day in the month of October in the year 3761 BCE. He turned on the lights and commenced to create the creation.

---

23 Britannica, T. Editors of Encyclopaedia. "anno mundi." Encyclopedia Britannica, October 11, 2013. https://www.britannica.com/topic/anno-mundi

Keep in mind that the calculation is that the creation happened under six thousand years ago—5784, to be exact, as of 2023. And in order to believe that this calculation is accurate, one must reject all known modern scientific geological dating methods while embracing the belief that the deity of the Bible created man pretty much in his present form as *Homo sapiens*, instantly fully developed, in one day, under six thousand years ago, again while ignoring the fossil data scientifically dating the human species at over two million years old, starting with *Homo habilis*. The anno mundi calculation for the day, month, and year of the creation of the world is based on the chronology of the creation story given in the Bible, in the book of Genesis, starting with Adam, a man who was created from the dust of the ground, and Eve, a woman who was brought forth into existence from a rib bone of that man named Adam.

The biblical timeline from the creation of Adam on day six to Noah at the time of the flood calculates to approximately 1,656 years, and continuing to Abraham and King David equates to approximately four thousand years before said birth of Christ, which most scholars approximate as between 6 and 4 BCE. From the birth of Christ until today, we are looking at a little over two thousand years based on this calculation.

What is truly interesting here is that there is no definitive physical or archaeological evidence for the existence of any of these biblical figures, up to and including Jesus the Christ—that is, a Jesus Christ that performed miracles and rose from the dead. Also, outside the biblical accounts, there is no secular historicity for any of these Bible greats. In fairness, I must state that we should understand that the average citizens of any past era rarely left behind any archaeological trails or made it into the pages of history, but are we going to define these men as such? Surely these specific men of the biblical text do not fall into the category of commoners, for we have Adam, claimed to be the first man to ever exist, thus the father of all humanity. A human that did not arrive into existence through natural birth but who was instantly pulled from the dust of the ground by God himself, and the only man ever to have come into being in this manner still to this day!

Then we have the righteous one named Noah. The Bible story is that Noah was the only living man on earth before the flood who still believed in, worshipped, and loved God. Imagine that: there was a time when there was only one living man on earth, Noah, who believed in the biblical God. Therefore, this God decided to destroy all humankind and the animals, too, to cleanse the earth, for the world had become too wicked and evil. God came to Noah, for he was the last righteous man left on earth, who was at the ripe old age of about five hundred or six hundred years. He was instructed by the Christian deity to build the ark to save himself and his family and to take one male and one female of every land animal to repopulate the earth after the destruction, for God promised to destroy everything that breathed. Yet Noah, like Adam, didn't make the history books, and actually, according to the Bible, Noah lived longer than Adam and was fifty years short of one thousand years old when he died! Further, around said time of this worldwide flood, great civilizations like those of the Egyptians, Mesopotamians, Sumerians, and others penned not one sentence about this claimed worldwide cataclysm in the pages of their history texts! One of the most puzzling omissions, also obviously by historians, has to be that huge ark! This had to have been the largest sea vessel in the world at that time and still would be one of the largest today if archaeologists could ever locate it, but it would be challenging to locate mythical sea vessels. It's puzzling that archaeologists can find the tooth of a million-year-old *Homo habilis* deep underground in a cave yet cannot find Noah's gigantic ark.

Next up we have Abraham, also known as the father of many nations. Abraham is the central figure and the patriarch of Judaism, Christianity, and Islam, thus the term *Abrahamic religions*. Abraham is considered the founding father of the Jewish nation of Israel. Jews believe that God made a special covenant with Abraham and that he and his descendants were the chosen people of God who would create a great nation. *Encyclopedia Britannica* is gracious with its position regarding Abraham's historicity. It states the following under its "The Critical Problem of a 'Biography' of Abraham" section: "There can be no biography of Abraham in the ordinary sense." [24] Whereas Wikipedia states the following: "Most historians view the patriarchal age, along with the Exodus and the period of the biblical judges, as a late literary construct that does not relate to any particular historical era; and after a century of exhaustive archaeological investigation, no evidence has been found for a historical Abraham." [25]

These three men of the Bible are pillars of the Christian faith; therefore, proving that even one of them is a myth sends the Christian faith tumbling to the ground. Fact: there is not a shred of secular independent evidence for the existence of Adam, Noah, or Abraham outside the Bible, historically or archaeologically!

Let's continue with King David. There are actually a few historians that agree that David probably existed around 1000 BCE, but there is little else that is agreed on about him as a historical figure. Until the recent discovery of a broken inscribed stone, now known as the Tel Dan Stele, in 1993, there was no evidence outside the Bible for the existence of King David. King David is not mentioned in any Egyptian, Syrian, or Assyrian record of the time, but with the Tel Dan Stele discovery and the Mesha Stele and a tenth-century Egyptian palace inscription, at least King David has some circumstantial evidence working in his favor to confirm him as a real historical figure. But then again, even with these three interpretations of mentions of King David, it is not a closed case, for not all the finds have been accepted as clear evidence by many scholars. The Tel Dan Stele is considered a work of forgery by some and seen as having been misinterpreted; the interpretation of the Mesha Stele's inscription by some scholars as referring to King David is countered by other experts, who believe that the inscription should be correctly interpreted as referring to King Balak. Others, like

24   Andre Parrot, "Abraham Hebrew patriarch", Encyclopedia Britannica, October 18, 2022, https://www.britannica.com/biography/Abraham

25   Wikipedia, "Abraham," January 23 2023, https://en.wikipedia.org/wiki/Abraham#:~:text=Most%20historians%20view%20the%20patriarchal,found%20for%20a%20historical%20Abraham.

Thomas L. Thompson, a biblical scholar and theologian, believe that the inscription on the Mesha Stele is not historical but an allegory. And finally, the tenth-century Egyptian inscription allegedly authenticating King David's name is more difficult than the one on the Mesha Stele, for much of the inscription is damaged and illegible, according to experts. Therefore, what is one to conclude from these three highly contentious and controversial discoveries? Ultimately none of the three discoveries definitively proves that King David existed.

Now, let us turn to the biblical Jesus, definitely the greatest figure of the Bible, who is regarded by most Christians as the incarnation of God. Yet we must ask here, also, Was Jesus the Christ a real divine historical person? Outside the four Gospels of the New Testament and other biblical or religious texts, what historical writings are there of this man deemed the son of God? The two most prominent non-Christian historians who have writings about Jesus attributed to them that are used to establish proof of the historicity of Jesus include the Jewish source Titus Flavius Josephus, born Yosef ben Matityahu, and the Roman source Publius Cornelius Tacitus. Jesus is said to have born circa 6–4 BCE in Bethlehem and to have died circa 30 CE in Jerusalem. Josephus was born circa 37 CE and died circa 100 CE, and the Roman Tacitus was born circa 56 CE and died circa 120 CE.

As one can see, both of these historians were born after the death of Jesus and would not have been capable of providing a firsthand account of a divine historical Jesus. So where did both historians get their information regarding Jesus? Josephus's manuscripts of the book *Antiquities of the Jews* contain two references to Jesus. The first reference, known as the Testimonium Flavianum, reads as follows:

> Now there was about this time Jesus, a wise man, if it be lawful to call him a man, for he was a doer of wonderful works, a teacher of such men as receive the truth with pleasure. He drew over to him both many of the Jews, and many of the Gentiles. He was the Christ, and when Pilate, at the suggestion of the principal men among us, had condemned him to

the cross, those that loved him at the first did not forsake him; for he appeared to them alive again the third day; as the divine prophets had foretold these and ten thousand other wonderful things concerning him. And the tribe of Christians so named from him are not extinct at this day. [26]

Most scholars believe that this passage is not authentic and is the work of Christian interpolations. Scholars note that Josephus was not a Christian, and so it is highly unlikely that he would have used phrases such as "if it be lawful to call him a man" or "he was the Christ." The vast majority of scholars of early Judaism and experts on the writings of Josephus believe this was likely touched up or forged by Christian scribes at a later time. Instead, it is asserted that the passage probably read like this:

Now, there was about this time Jesus, a wise man; for he was a doer of wonderful works, a teacher of such men as receive the truth with pleasure. He drew over to him both many of the Jews and many of the Gentiles. And when Pilate, at the suggestion of the principal men among us, had condemned him to the cross, those that loved him at the first ceased not so to do; and the race of Christians, so named from him, are not extinct even now. [27]

Furthermore, many skeptics argue that Josephus actually made no references to Jesus at all and that both mentions of him were added by Christians.

Josephus mentions Jesus a second time, in book 20:

But the younger Ananus who, as we said, received the high priesthood, was of a bold disposition and exceptionally daring; he followed the party of the Sadducees, who are severe in judgment above all the Jews, as we have already shown. As therefore Ananus was of such a disposition, he thought he had now a good opportunity, as Festus was now dead, and Albinus was still on the road; so he assembled a council of

26   Jon Sorensen, "Is This Mention of Jesus a Forgery?," Catholic Answers, December 07, 2021, https://www.catholic.com/magazine/online-edition/is-this-mention-of-jesus-a-forgery.
27   Jon Sorensen, "Is This Mention of Jesus a Forgery?," Catholic Answers, December 07, 2021, https://www.catholic.com/magazine/online-edition/is-this-mention-of-jesus-a-forgery.

judges, and brought before it the brother of Jesus the so-called Christ, whose name was James, together with some others, and having accused them as lawbreakers, he delivered them over to be stoned. [28]

Many scholars view this second mention of Jesus, unlike the first mention of Jesus by Josephus, as untouched by Christian interpolations, while others view Josephus's writings about Jesus as entirely Christian forgeries.

Publius Cornelius Tacitus, the Roman historian and politician, wrote this in a passage from *The Annals*:

But all human efforts, all the lavish gifts of the emperor, and the propitiations of the gods, did not banish the sinister belief that the conflagration was the result of an order. Consequently, to get rid of the report, Nero fastened the guilt and inflicted the most exquisite tortures on a class hated for their abominations, called Christians by the populace. Christus, from whom the name had its origin, suffered the extreme penalty during the reign of Tiberius at the hands of one of our procurators, Pontius Pilatus, and a most mischievous superstition, thus checked for the moment, again broke out not only in Judæa, the first source of the evil, but even in Rome, where all things hideous and shameful from every part of the world find their centre and become popular. Accordingly, an arrest was first made of all who pleaded guilty; then, upon their information, an immense multitude was convicted, not so much of the crime of firing the city, as of hatred against mankind. [29]

One must ask whether these are Christian claims merely being repeated or whether Tacitus had access to independent sources regarding "Christus" and the Christians, for Tacitus was not alive when the described event occurred, nor was Tacitus alive when Jesus lived; therefore, this is not a firsthand account nor the confirmation of a divine historical Jesus the Christ.

28 Evan Minton, "DID JESUS EXIST?," Cross Examined, August 29, 2019, https://crossexamined. org/did-jesus-exist/.

29 Tacitus, "The Internet Classics Archive: The Annals by Tacitus," January 20, 2023, http://classics. mit.edu/Tacitus/annals.11.xv.html

Now, what is one to conclude here? For this writing does not equate to legitimate historicity but rather is merely stating a story secondhand at best. If a highly respected, prominent, modern-day historian made reference to one or two of Spider-Man's great comic book adventures in his or her written work today, would this prove to those who would read these writings five hundred years from now that Spider-Man was a real historical figure with superpowers?

The tenuous evidence for Jesus being a divine historical figure grows even more doubtful when Gaius Caecilius Cilo, better known as Pliny the Younger, who was a Roman author and administrator, is added into the "proof" bowl of evidence. Pliny was born circa 61 CE and died circa 113 CE. While interrogating Christians, Pliny described their practices by writing the following: "They were in the habit of meeting on a certain fixed day before it was light, when they sang in alternate verses a hymn to Christ, as to a god, and bound themselves by a solemn oath, not to any wicked deeds, but never to commit any fraud, theft or adultery, never to falsify their word, nor deny a trust when they should be called upon to deliver it up; after which it was their custom to separate, and then reassemble to partake of food—but food of an ordinary and innocent kind." [30] Pliny's letter here was seeking counsel or advice on dealing with the early Christian community, for he was conducting trials of suspected Christians. Pliny states that he gave Christians multiple chances to affirm they were innocent, but if they refused three times, they were killed. The letter (Epistulae X.96), written circa 112 CE, does not attest to the historicity of biblical Jesus; it reveals only how Christians practiced their faith during that era. How does this writing prove Jesus was God in the flesh? A better question would be, Why didn't Pliny the Elder write of Jesus?

Then we have Gaius Suetonius Tranquillus, known as Suetonius, who was born circa 69 CE and died circa 122 CE. He was a Roman biographer and antiquarian. Suetonius possibly mentions Christ briefly

---

30 Michael Gleghorn, "Ancient Evidence for Jesus from Non-Christian Sources," Probe Ministries, December 26, 2022, https://probe.org/ancient-evidence-for-jesus-from-non-christian-sources-2/

in the fifth volume of *Lives of the Twelve Caesars*, written around 120 CE: "Since the Jews constantly made disturbances at the instigation of Chrestus, he [the emperor Claudius] expelled them from Rome." Research shows that the word *Chrestus* was common at the time, particularly for slaves, and meant *good* or *useful*. This writing was almost a century after the biblical Jesus's death and does not provide or serve as clear evidence for the historicity of Jesus, for there is not even scholarly certainty on whether this writing is even about the Jesus of the Bible.

Let's summarize these "secular" writings about Jesus the Christ. Neither Josephus nor Tacitus nor Pliny nor Suetonius lived during the time of Jesus; therefore, all their writings pertaining to him are, at best, hearsay. Absolutely none of these writings afford us firsthand accounts. Further, there are no known firsthand accounts of the historicity of Jesus by other historians who were alive during the time of Jesus.

In addition to the absence of firsthand accounts, the writings of Josephus and Tacitus are also known to have been altered by Christian interpolation. Such a nice-sounding phrase, "Christian interpolation," but many scholars would rather have it called what it really is: forgery. For the alterations are believed by many to be not accidental but clever attempts by Christians to write Jesus into history, which renders the writings unreliable, in the opinion of many. Tacitus's celebrated passage on Jesus is considered by many scholars to be forgery or interpolation. Further, the first publication of any part of the *Annals* of Tacitus was by Johannes de Spire in Venice in the year 1468! Prior to 1468 the general public did not know of these writings. Really think about that fact for a moment. The forgery of Josephus's writing on Jesus is so obvious that even Christian apologists agree that it was altered. This makes the entire passage by Josephus about Jesus suspect. Josephus, considered a traitor, had a great relationship with members of the Flavian dynasty, who ruled the Roman Empire. These were Vespasian (who reigned 69–79) and his sons Titus (79–81) and Domitian (81–96). Those who believe that Jesus was an invention by the Romans to promote a more peaceful messiah who would suppress further uprisings against Rome also believe that Josephus, who, as mentioned earlier, was born Yosef ben Matityahu and changed his name to Titus Flavius Josephus, defected and became an adviser to Titus to assist in creating what we now know as the New Testament. If this claim is ever proved, all writings on Jesus by Josephus should be rejected. The writings of Pliny and Suetonius, just like those of Josephus and Tacitus, do not deliver any firsthand accounts of miracles or divinity; thus, there is no credible history of Jesus the Christ outside the Bible.

The ultimate goal of this writing is not to disrespect the Bible or its characters, but we must aggressively scrutinize its claims if we are truly to discover the reliability of it. The name Jesus (or Yeshua; the letter *J* wasn't invented until the 1500s) was a popular name at the time. Also, there were many self-proclaimed saviors during this time and the time of the biblical Jesus, and the penalty of crucifixion was also a popular means of execution. So it's possible that a "Jesus," or Yeshua, was crucified—even perhaps the Jesus of the Bible. But even if the Jesus of the Bible existed and was charismatic enough to separate himself from the many other "saviors," he was not of divine origin, he did not perform the claimed miracles in the Bible, and he did not return from death. For if such a man lived, I ask you, why is there no firsthand account of him by any historian of that time? In other words, there is no proof.

Further, I am of the opinion that attempting to prove the historicity of Jesus the Christ is comparable to attempting to prove the historicity of Santa Claus. The fairy-tale Santa Claus of today evolved from the Dutch legend of Sinterklaas, who was an older man who dressed as a bishop and brought Dutch children presents in early December. Sinterklaas is actually based on the historical figure of Saint Nicholas of Myra. The historical Saint Nicholas was known for his regular tendency for secret gift-giving. This gave rise to the modern-day model of Saint Nicholas, known worldwide as Santa Claus, through Sinterklaas. So just as there were men named Yeshua, there was a man named Saint Nicholas, but neither Saint Nicholas nor the Jesus of the Bible had supernatural powers.

Again, the Jesus of the Bible was no man of divine origin. He did not perform claimed miracles stated in the Bible, and he did not die and return from death, much the way Saint Nicholas was not capable of traveling across the entire globe and delivering presents to every good child within an eight- to ten-hour period; nor did the latter have eight magical reindeer and one special lead magical reindeer with a bright, illuminated red shiny nose, all of which were capable of flying. Saint Nicholas did not have the ability to fit himself and others through any chimneys with presents in tow without catching on fire and could not levitate back up a chimney after dropping off toys made by magical elves that were immortal and possessed magical powers; these also never existed.

So here we are attempting to understand the origins of time and of humanity. We also attempt to examine the biblical timeline, which involves the genealogy in Genesis, in an effort to understand the rabbinic calculations of anno mundi, yet we cannot locate any secular historical evidence for any of the giants of the Bible, including its main character, Jesus the Christ. If it is true that creation is under six thousand years old, how is it that Christians cannot identify the location of the Garden of Eden, where Adam was said to have been created, yet archaeologists can identify some of the earliest cave dwellings of the human species, even some that are two million years old? Scientists can take us to observe a sixty-seven-thousand-year-old metatarsal, or toe bone, of an early human species, yet Christians cannot show us the remains of the ark that was built by a six-hundred-year-old Noah to the size of three hundred cubits long, fifty cubits wide, and thirty cubits high—a vessel almost larger than the *Titanic*, yet archaeologists have never found the remains of such a huge vessel? Abraham left us without any archaeological or secular historical evidence for Christians to show us that he existed, yet scientists can take us to forty-two-thousand-year-old tiny jewelry beads constructed from animal teeth by the Neanderthals? No Christian can bring us the crown of King David, yet archaeologists can bring us the skull of a *Homo erectus* dating 1.8 million years old. No Christian can show us the blood from the cross Jesus is said to have been executed on, yet scientists can show us the oldest human DNA, dating back hundreds of thousands of years. Where is the evidence, and how is it possible that there is none? Yet the anno mundi is based on the biblical chronology starting with Adam, the man who the Bible claims was created straight from the ground, fully formed.

Millions of Christians and Jews believe that the earth and the universe are both only six thousand years old, but scientists believe that the universe about 13.8 billion years old and the planet Earth is about 4.6 billion years old. How can Christians and scientists be so far apart in their calculations? Well, let's compare both methods of calculation. The Christians simply use what I like to refer to as the Adam-and-Eve-based *begation* method drawn from the book of Genesis. This method gave us the anno mundi calculation used by the Jews, while scientists use methods described on the International Planetarium Society page, which states the following:

> The age of the Earth is measured by studies of radioactive elements. Radioactive elements are unstable and "parent" atoms decay into other "daughter" elements at a steady rate. For example, through a series of steps, atoms of uranium decay into atoms of lead. By measuring the abundance of "parent" and "daughter" atoms in rock samples and knowing the decay rate, geologists can calculate the age of the rock. Using several different sets of parent and daughter elements, geologists have measured the age of a variety of rocks, including terrestrial and lunar rocks as well as meteorites, which originate primarily from asteroids. The results consistently indicate an age of about 4.56 billion years for the Earth.

> The age of the Universe is measured in several ways. One method is based on the rate of expansion of the Universe. By measuring the distance to remote galaxies and the rate at which they are expanding away from us, astronomers can calculate how much time the galaxies have needed to get as far away as they are.

This tells how long the Universe has been expanding, or how old it is. These studies yield an age of about 13.8 billion years.

The age of the Universe can also be determined by investigating the oldest clusters of stars. This is done by measuring the brightness and temperature of stars in a cluster and comparing those measurements with models of how the brightness and temperature of a star change as the star ages. It is somewhat like estimating the age of a person by looking at features of his or her face and knowing how our faces change as we age. These studies show that the oldest star clusters are about 12 billion years old. The Universe must be older than its stars, so this method establishes a minimum age for the Universe. Similar studies show that the Sun is about 5 billion years old, consistent with the age of the Earth measured by radioactive studies. A third way to determine the age of the Universe involves measuring the ages of long-lived dying stars. As stars like the Sun age, they eventually become very small, faint objects about the size of the Earth. These stellar corpses are called "white dwarf" stars and have no remaining sources of new energy. Astronomers can calculate the rate at which white dwarfs get fainter and cooler, so when they then measure the brightness and temperature of a white dwarf star, they can recognize how old it is. These studies show that the oldest white dwarf stars are at least 10 billion years old. As above, this establishes a minimum age for the Universe since the Universe must be older than its stars. [31]

Which of these approaches for determining the age of the universe and the planet is more likely to be accurate? The calculation that is based on the biblical chronology of men for whom no verifiable archaeological or historical evidence exists to prove that they ever lived, thus rendering no trace of historicity, or the calculations based on scientific methods and protocols? If one had a six-week-old son or daughter in the hospital

---

31   International Planetarium Society, "Position Statement: Age of the Earth and Universe - Planetarium," January 21, 2023, https://www.ips-planetarium.org/page/age

in need of open-heart surgery, which doctor would one select to per-form the operation, the man or woman with a Bible, a PhD in theology, and the belief that God would guide his or her hand in the operating room or the trained surgeon who had a master of surgery degree? Here we are attempting to determine the age of the universe and of creation, which includes our planet. Are we to trust a rabbinic calculation based on a book written by men who once believed that the sun revolved around planet Earth, or will we embrace the scientific calculations based on empirical evidence as closer to the truth?

Again, I must repeat that the rabbinic calculations for anno mundi put all creation at under six thousand years old. How plausible is this calculation when compared to calculations that are testable explana-tions and predictions backed by scientific research methodologies? In the preface of this book, I refenced the age-old question, How is it that we be? If biblical experts are calculating under six thousand years as the age of all creation, which obviously cannot be correct, then the Bible would have to be dismissed as a reliable tool for answering the questions of the origins of time and of humankind. Anno mundi cal-culations are based on the biblical chronology of men who are, by sec-ular experts' assessments, regarded generally as mythical figures in the book of Genesis, which is a piece of writing accredited to Moses, who is also generally regarded as a myth. What, then, are we to make of this book called the Bible when it obviously is incapable of providing sound, reasonable explanations for the origins of time and life? What other purpose might it serve?

Many, if not most, Christians would say that one of the primary purposes of the Bible is that it serves as a source of instructions for the deliverance from sin—or, in other words, the Bible can be viewed as a manual used for salvation by those who choose to believe in its claims and requirements. What, then, is sin, and why do we need deliverance from it?

CHAPTER 4

Born of Sin

*And the Lord God commanded the man, saying, of every
tree of the garden thou mayest freely eat: But of the tree of
the knowledge of good and evil, thou shalt not eat of it: for
in the day that thou eatest thereof thou shalt surely die.*
—*Genesis 2:16–17*

According to the Bible, a woman named Eve, a man named Adam, a forbidden fruit, and a talking snake that also walked contributed to the "fall of man." When Eve and Adam ate of the forbidden fruit from the tree of knowledge of good and evil after being tricked by a talking snake, the original sin is said to have been committed, thus ending immortality for all living creations on earth. God punished them by driving them out of the garden. The omniscient deity of the Christian Bible placed a forbidden tree, the tree of the knowledge of good and evil, in the middle of the garden called Eden, knowing that Adam and Eve would eat from it and that all humanity would suffer consequences resulting from their actions. Why would an infinitely wise and loving God permit this to unfold?

Two people, Adam and Eve, ate of the forbidden fruit, according to the Bible, and the biblical all-loving God punished all unborn humanity and every living thing on earth. This Bible story makes the biblical God the antithesis of all loving. Also, is knowledge not good? Why wouldn't God want Adam and Eve to have knowledge of good and evil, considering God was allowing Lucifer, the epitome of evil, to enter into the Garden of Eden, or at least the serpent, which is described as the most intelligent of all the wild animals that God had made, even if the serpent was not Lucifer—yet God didn't want Adam and Eve to have knowledge of good and evil?

Let us look deeper into this supposed account of the fall of man. Again, the previous chapters of this book have demonstrated that the Bible is not a reliable or sound source of information for answering the questions regarding the origins of time or the genesis of humankind in a rational and factual manner. Therefore, we now seek to understand the Bible's purpose as it pertains to salvation, which is the deliverance of Christians from sin. Sin is defined as the transgression of the "divine" law or disobedience toward God in the realm of religion, or simply missing the mark. According to the Christian faith, we are born sinners! Before we take our first breaths of air, before we take our first steps as infants, before we utter our first words, according to the Bible, we are all morally defective, born with the affliction called sin.

Sin, moral evil as considered from a religious standpoint or a transgression against divine law. Those who do not embrace God as a reality view the concept of "sin" as an invention by humanity, an imaginary and nonexistent "transgression" against a man-made invented character (i.e., God) who is also well, nonexistent. Sin is a religious concept. The belief in sin requires belief in a deity that is a supernatural being and the object of worship.

So when Eve and Adam ate from the tree of knowledge of good and evil, the affliction of sin was extended to all humanity, which should be troubling, for why would a loving, just, and forgiving God punish all humankind for the acts of two people? Adam and Eve were the only humans in the Garden of Eden. No one else was alive to eat from the forbidden tree; therefore, no one else committed any wrongdoing, yet God punished the unborn along with Adam and Eve.

Considering the gravity of what this infraction would mean to the innocent unborn, why wasn't God loving enough to give Adam and Eve another chance or just enough to punish only Adam and Eve, or even forgiving enough to simply forgive them?

Psalm 51:1 reads, "But you, Lord, are a compassionate and gracious God, slow to anger, abounding in love and faithfulness." When Adam and Eve committed the "original sin," was God having a bad day? For God's response to Adam's and Eve's actions contradicts that verse and all other biblical verses that describe the Christian God as compassionate, loving, and forgiving! The Christian deity is described as a god that is omniscient (all-knowing), omnipotent (all-powerful), and omnibenevolent (supremely good). This translates to God knowing everything, God having the power to do anything, and God being perfectly good. The three Os were not present in the "original sin" story! God supposedly knows everything yet still did not come up with a better plan to prevent the failed outcome in the Garden of Eden. God supposedly is all-powerful yet did nothing to prevent the serpent from interacting with Eve. God is supposedly perfectly good yet punished all humankind for the actions of two people—two people who could not differentiate between good and evil until they ate the so-called forbidden fruit! The "original sin" story and the explanations given by Christians and apologists who argue desperately to rationalize this tale are truly an assault on one's logic and reasoning.

Let us probe even deeper into the tale. A major player in the original sin story, of course, is the snake or serpent. One interpretation of the Bible is that Satan entered the body of the serpent to tempt Eve. Why was Satan allowed into Eden, God's perfect paradise for humankind, after being cast from heaven for falling into sin and taking a third of God's angels with him? Satan, regarded as the epitome of evil and author of sin, an angel who rebelled against God in heaven in an attempt to become equal to him, was permitted by God to enter Eden. Satan, originally known as Lucifer, was created as a perfect, wise, and beautiful angel but sinned in heaven in the presence of God himself and also apparently a third of God's other angels as well—angels, I say—yet Adam and Eve were expected to fare better on earth, in the Garden of Eden, against the powers of Satan as their adversary when God himself could not keep heaven sinless? Adam and Eden were not created perfect, like Lucifer; also, they were not angels with supernatural powers, only humans. In fact, Adam and Eve had no knowledge of good and evil, nor did they know that they were naked, yet Lucifer, who was created as the perfect angel with supernatural powers, sinned in heaven in the presence of God. How was this even possible?

The original sin, incredibly, took place in heaven and not in the Garden of Eden. 1 John 3:8 reads, "He that committeth sin is of the devil; for the devil sinneth from the beginning. For this purpose, the Son of God was manifested, that he might destroy the works of the devil." The fact that the biblical God created Adam and Eve without the ability to distinguish between good and evil yet allowed the highest-ranked angel ever created, an angel turned villain who was so powerful that a third of God's very own angels joined his team, access to two innocent, ignorant, and vulnerable naked people in the Garden of Eden while the fate of all of humankind hung in the balance is utterly incomprehensible to the reasonable mind. This act of the all-knowing God is akin to letting a pedophile Catholic priest have free rein in a children's day care center. The angel Lucifer, who was created perfect in heaven, sinned in heaven; God created Adam and Eve as human beings with insufficient knowledge and awareness, yet God was looking for a better outcome?

In order for one to accept the original sin story as factual, one must put aside reality as we know it and actually believe that a reptile, and in this case a snake, walked up to Eve—yes, walked, for apparently before the Christian God cursed it, snakes walked as well as talked; the language in which they spoke is not specified in the book of Genesis, but whatever language it was, it was the same as Eve's; thus, when approached, Eve was not stricken with fear that a walking, talking reptile was engaging her in verbal conversation! The snake sauntered up to Eve and spoke intelligently with her in Genesis 3:1–5 as follows:

"Now the serpent was more subtil than any beast of the field which the Lord God had made. And he said unto the woman, Yea, hath God said, Ye shall not eat of every tree of the garden? And the woman said unto the serpent, we may eat of the fruit of the trees of the garden: But of the fruit of the tree which is in the midst of the garden, God hath said, Ye shall not eat of it, neither shall ye touch it, lest ye die. And the serpent said unto the woman, Ye shall not surely die: For God doth know that in the day ye eat thereof, then your eyes shall be opened, and ye shall be as gods, knowing good and evil."

The snake not only spoke but reasoned with Eve. This snake walked, talked, and reasoned with a human being! Think about how incredible that account is, yet everything the serpent stated was true! Adam and Eve did not die on that very day of eating the fruit, and their eyes were opened; therefore, they gained the knowledge of good and evil!

Outside the Bible there has never been a report or discovery of any human who has ever had a conversation with a talking snake—well, not any sane person, that is, but then again, this was not your regular reptile. Some Christians will argue that it was the devil, or Lucifer, the angel gone bad, who possessed the body of the reptile, and that's how it was made possible for the snake to talk. In the original sin story, the snake either was an animal that was capable of speech and acted alone in tricking Eve or was not capable of talking, which would support the narrative that Lucifer possessed it to trick Eve. If the talking snake acted alone and was indeed a crafty reptile who was not possessed by Lucifer, the devil, and it deceived Eve, then God is on record for punishing it alone, as stated in Genesis 3:14–15, which reads as follows: "And the Lord God said unto the serpent, because thou hast done this, thou art cursed above all cattle, and above every beast of the field; upon thy belly shalt thou go, and dust shalt thou eat all the days of thy life: And I will put enmity between thee and the woman, and between thy seed and her seed; it shall bruise thy head, and thou shalt bruise his heel."

It's interesting to note here that God never spoke of cursing the snake never to be able to talk again, for one would think this was one of the curses, since there are no known species of talking snakes in existence today. But if the snake was possessed by Lucifer, why did God curse the powerless reptile if the all-knowing God knew that it was actually Lucifer who tricked Eve into eating the forbidden fruit, thereby committing the sin? When the omniscient, omnipotent, and omnibenevolent God came trudging through the garden, calling out and asking where everybody was and what everyone had done, Adam threw Eve under the bus by saying it was the woman who gave him the fruit. As he pointed her out, Eve said the snake beguiled her. As she pointed the snake out, now, if the snake could talk, would it not have spoken up to defend itself by proclaiming "The devil made me do it"? Why would the talking snake remain silent when it had the ability of verbal communication? Now, if snakes never ever had the ability to talk, and this snake spoke only because the devil possessed it, wouldn't God have seen the devil running out of town when he showed up?

Matthew 5:48 states, "Be ye therefore perfect, even as your Father which is in heaven is perfect." The Bible clearly states that God is perfect. One could assume that a flawless god's work would be flawless or perfect as well, and one would assume correctly, for the "inspired" word states so in Deuteronomy 32:4: "He is the Rock, his work is perfect: for all his ways are judgment: a god of truth and without iniquity, just and right is he." One need not be an astrophysicist to understand the claims made here, for there is very little room for misinterpretation. These verses are describing the Christian deity as a perfect being who produces only perfect work, a deity that is flawless, who does no wrong and who is without iniquity. The perfect God of the biblical texts saw his work during the creation of the world as good on multiple occasions: Genesis 1:4, Genesis 1:10, Genesis 1:12, Genesis 1:18, Genesis 1:21, and Genesis 1:25, and when the perfect God finally completed all the work, not only did he see it as good; God also saw it as very good, as stated in Genesis 1:31, "And God saw everything that he had made, and, behold, it was very good. And the evening and the morning were the sixth day."

Yet the perfect omniscient God of the Bible knew that his most beautiful and perfectly created angel, Lucifer, would sin in heaven, of all places, and become his evil archrival for all eternity. Also, those two people that he had placed in the Garden of Eden, Adam and Eve, were about to introduce death and curse the world—including all humanity not yet born, the animal kingdom, and plant life and insects—with the consequences of their actions, for the interpretation is that before the fall of man, everything that had life was immortal. This perfect God who is described as omnibenevolent and without iniquity not only punished the innumerable humans not yet born for the actions of two ignorant and innocent people who ate a fruit; he also included house cats, turtles, rabbits, goldfish, butterflies, praying mantises, ants, cacti, and tulips—or, in other words, every living thing, even that which was incapable of sin! The biblical deity was so angry that he cursed the ground in Genesis 3:17–18 which reads, "And unto Adam he said, because thou hast hearkened unto the voice of thy wife, and hast eaten of the tree, of which I commanded thee, saying, thou shalt not eat of it: cursed is the ground for thy sake; in sorrow shalt thou eat of it all the days of thy life; Thorns also and thistles shall it bring forth to thee; and thou shalt eat the herb of the field."

How could this be seen as good, with this fate pending? How is the biblical God perfect when his perfectly created angel Lucifer was made capable of sin? How was God's earthly creation seen as good when the devil was about to enter the Garden of Eden, and how could this biblical God, said to be without iniquity, punish you and me for the actions of two people we never knew? This is not goodness nor perfection; this is madness, for it is grossly unfair to punish all humanity for the actions of two people, even more so two people who were not fully awake consciously, not knowing the difference between good and evil, and tricked by a supernatural being—Lucifer, an angel that God himself expelled from his dwelling place in heaven—that was then allowed into humankind's dwelling place on earth for humankind to do battle with. Perhaps if there had been no talking snake to tempt Eve, there would be no sin, unless Eve ran into Balaam's talking ass.

The intellectual and rational being is charged with believing that humanity is now cursed and became sinful as the result of a talking, walking snake that hoodwinked a woman into eating a fruit that the biblical deity deemed off limits. This omnipotent, omnibenevolent, and omniscient deity had failed to keep heaven sinless with angels inhabiting it yet proceeded to create two ignorant humans on earth who didn't even know the difference between good and evil and expected them to do a better job than his heavenly angelic tenants. Psalm 18:30 reads, "As for God, his way is perfect: the word of the Lord is tried: he is a buckler to all those that trust in him." Before the original sin, earth knew not death, so once man ate of the forbidden fruit, death entered the world. The all-loving god of the Bible punished animals and plants and insects along with humanity! If animals can't sin, surely plants cannot. Why did God bring death upon them too? Shouldn't animals and plants and insects still be living for all eternity if Psalm 18:30 is accurate? And if animals, insects, and plants were not cursed by the original sin, then why do these things experience death if in the beginning the world did not know death? If Adam and Eve were in their original state of being prior to eating the forbidden fruit and were attempting to gain employment as educators at your local neighborhood high school today, they would not meet the requirements and would be deemed unfit for employment. If Adam and Eve today attempted to gain employment as security guards at any bonded security agency paying minimum wage, they would be found unfit or lacking the necessary psychological tools to make them ideal employees—or, in other words, because of their comprehension impairment, they would be unsuccessful at acquiring jobs as security officers. If Adam and Eve even wanted to apply for jobs as Sunday school teachers, would you hire them to work at your local church? If Adam and Eve applied for jobs as criminal attorneys today, no reputable firm would employ them. Yet the biblical God employed Adam and Eve with the most critical job description ever bestowed upon any humans before or since, and that job was to keep death and sin out of the world. The biblical God employed these two humans whom he had made ignorant and innocent, who did not have the capability of knowing the difference between good and evil. He assigned Adam and Eve as the gatekeepers to keep death and sin out of the world as the fate of all humanity and all creation hung in the balance? If the biblical deity really existed and wanted a perfect world without death and sin, it would be so, for one man or woman eating a fruit would not have ruined it, yet we have a story of a perfect God who cursed all creation because two people consumed some fruit.

In the Bible God told Adam directly not to eat of the forbidden fruit. One could assume that Eve learned of this information from Adam, for she states that eating from the tree of knowledge of good and evil was forbidden. Eve was tricked into eating the forbidden fruit, yet Adam took of the fruit without hesitation or reservation when Eve offered it to him, according to Genesis 3:6, "And when the woman saw that the tree was good for food, and that it was pleasant to the eyes, and a tree to be desired to make one wise, she took of the fruit thereof, and did eat, and gave also unto her husband with her; and he did eat." And because of this verse, the woman has been viewed for the last two thousand years as the root cause or initiator of the original sin or, in other words, the scapegoat. 1 Timothy 2:14 reads like a pardon for Adam, but in my attempt to remain fair and unbiased in my interpretation, I wish to present the full context of 1 Timothy 2:14 so that the reader can draw a greater interpretation from book, chapter, and verse; therefore, let us look at 1 Timothy 2:11–15 which reads, "Let the woman learn in silence with all subjection. But I suffer not a woman to teach, nor to usurp authority over the man, but to be in silence. For Adam was first formed, then Eve. And Adam was not deceived, but the woman being deceived was in the transgression.

Notwithstanding she shall be saved in childbearing, if they continue in faith and charity and holiness with sobriety."

For anyone who may be having any difficulty interpreting these verses, let us turn to the International Children's Bible and read from the identical book, chapter, and verses, which read, "A woman should learn by listening quietly and being fully ready to obey. I do not allow a woman to teach a man or to have authority over a man. She must remain silent. For Adam was made first; Eve was made later. Also, Adam was not the one who was tricked by the devil. It was the woman who was tricked and became a sinner. But women will be saved through having children. They will be saved if they continue in faith, love, holiness, and self-control." Here you have some of the most patriarchal language in the "inspired" biblical text. Apart from undermining the equality and dignity of women, 1 Timothy 2:14 reaffirms that Eve was the cause and means for the downfall of Adam and ultimately all humankind.

Although it is traditionally taught, and even stated in the Bible, that one man, or Adam, brought sin into the world, still, it is very clear, however, whom the Bible is also pointing the finger at for causing man to fail, thus bringing sin and death upon all of humankind: the woman called Eve, named by Adam, for Adam named all his subjects. Again, Lucifer committed the very first sin in all creation in heaven, and God cast him and the all the other sinful angels loyal to him out of heaven. One would hope that an all-loving God would punish only parties guilty of wrongdoing, for this is just, and it appears that God did so with angels in heaven, yet the biblical God did not afford humankind the same courtesy he afforded perfectly created angels in heaven.

Why didn't God curse the heavens or the other created living angels in heaven or those not yet created when Lucifer sinned against him in his presence yet cursed all humankind and all living things on earth, even the ground, when Adam and Eve sinned on earth while lacking knowledge? God saw fit to simply dispel Lucifer and a third of his angels from heaven; thus, heaven returned to its original sin-free state. There was no need for God to send himself (Jesus) to perform a sacrificial death for redemption. Further, no newly created angels were tainted with the heavenly original sin committed by Lucifer, for God obviously wanted heaven to remain sin-free and perfect.

One could argue that if God wanted the world and humankind to be sin-free and perfect, why didn't almighty God replicate the same solution on earth that he executed in heaven by simply expelling Adam and Eve from the world? According to the original sin story, God commanded the man, Adam, directly not to eat of the forbidden fruit yet never commanded the woman, Eve, to do likewise, knowing that the snake would test her and not Adam. It's strikingly odd that neither God nor Adam came to Eve's rescue when the talking snake came upon her. One could interpret this lack of action as God not really being that serious about a sin-free and immortal world. God did not intervene to stop sin, sickness, and death from entering the world yet took the time to interfere in many lesser affairs in the Bible. To mention only a few here, for example, in Joshua 10:12–14, God intervened when Joshua asked for the sun to be still so that he could have daylight to continue to fight and defeat his enemies. God also intervened when Balaam attempted to curse the people of Israel when Balaam was on the road to Moab. Stopping Balaam from making the trip to Moab was so important that God opened the mouth of the ass and gave it the ability to speak. I couldn't make this stuff up. Numbers 22:28 reads, "And the Lord opened the mouth of the ass, and she said unto Balaam, What have I done unto thee, that thou hast smitten me these three times?"

God also intervenes in the story of the Tower of Babel. The Babylonians wanted to become celebrated by building a mighty city and a tower. God disrupted the work by discombobulating the language of the workers so that they could no longer understand one another. The reason, apparently, was that God was troubled, for if they were successful in accomplishing this feat, nothing would be impossible for man to accomplish, as Genesis 11:3–9 describes! So God intervened for Joshua to win a battle, intervened in Balaam's trip to Moab to stop a curse, and intervened with the Babylonians to halt the construction of a tower, yet when the fate of humanity was hanging in the balance as a supernatural serpent was beguiling a half-witted Eve, the Christian God was silent as the greatest calamity in the Bible unfolded.

Today many Christians, if not most, believe that the world wouldn't be sinful and life would be immortal if it weren't for the woman—namely, Eve. Should Eve be viewed as the only culprit, as the initiator or gateway of the original sin? Shouldn't God have protected her, since he did not make her knowledgeable of good and evil? What if Eve had her day in a court of law with a fair and impartial judge and jury? Might she be exonerated?

CHAPTER 5

The Trial of Eve of Eden

The State of Humanity *v.* Eve
IN THE SUPREME COURT OF
the World

THE PEOPLE,
Plaintiff and Respondent,

v.

EVE,
Defendant and Appellant

Bailiff: All rise. The Supreme Court of the First Judicial Circuit, Transgressions Division, is now in session, the Honorable Judge Jack Daniels presiding.

Judge: Good morning, ladies and gentlemen. Everyone but the jury may be seated. Will the clerk please swear in the jury? Also, due to the sensitive nature of this hearing, let's leave out the "so help you God."

Clerk: Will the jury please raise your right hands? Does each of you swear that you will fairly try the case before this court and that you will return a true verdict according to the evidence and the instructions of the court? Please say "I do."

Jurors: I do.

Clerk: You may be seated.

Judge: Members of the jury, your duty today will be to determine whether the defendant is guilty or not guilty based only on facts and evidence provided in this case. The prosecution must prove that a transgression was committed and that the defendant is the person who committed the transgression. However, if you are not satisfied of the defendant's guilt to that extent, then reasonable doubt exists, and the defendant must be found not guilty. Bailiff, what is today's case?

Bailiff: Your Honor, today's case is the State of Humanity versus Eve of Eden.

Judge: Is the prosecution ready?

Prosecutor: Ready for the people, Your Honor.

Judge: Is the defense ready?

Eve: Ready for the defense, Your Honor.

Judge: Ms. Eve, are you without legal counsel or a defense attorney today?

Eve: Your Honor, no one defended me in the Garden of Eden; therefore, I've chosen to defend myself outside it.

Judge: Very well then. [*Gives the prosecution team the nod to begin.*]

Opening Statements

District Attorney: [*Stands up and speaks to the jury.*] Your Honor and ladies and gentlemen of the jury, the defendant has been charged with the offense of committing the original sin that led to the fall of humanity. The defendant alone is to blame and no one else, for the defendant ate of the forbidden fruit first, then gave some to her husband, Adam, who also did eat of the forbidden fruit. The defendant's self-serving actions led not only her husband, Adam, into sin but also all descendants of Adam, for from the moment he ate of the forbidden fruit, all human beings would be born into sin! It was the defendant who fantasized about how good the forbidden fruit would taste. The defendant found the forbidden fruit to be beautiful, and the defendant craved the wisdom that the forbidden fruit might bring to her.

The evidence I present will prove to you that the defendant is guilty as charged.

If I may, I would like to quote one of the greatest philosophers who ever lived, Aristotle, who once stated that "the cause of a cause is the cause of that which is caused." In other words, it can be emphatically stated that Adam's fall was caused by Eve's transgression, first against God, resulting in the original sin! God confirms this himself in Genesis 3:17, which states, "And unto Adam He [God] said, "Because thou hast hearkened unto the voice of thy wife [Eve], and hast eaten of the tree of which I commanded thee [Adam], saying, 'Thou shalt not eat of it,' cursed is the ground for thy sake; in sorrow shalt thou eat of it all the days of thy life." Further, the defendant has already confessed to the transgression, and this evidence will be presented shortly to quickly wrap up this trial, for as far as I see it, this is an open-and-shut case. The evidence I'll present will prove to you that the defendant is guilty as charged.

Eve: [*Stands up and speaks to the jury.*] Your Honor and ladies and gentlemen of the jury, under the law I am presumed innocent until proved guilty. During this trial, you will hear no real evidence that would render me culpable of the charges that are being brought against me. You will come to know the truth that perhaps I was a pawn and scapegoat, or, to be blunt, the expendable woman in this all-male patriarchal story—hell, even the devil was male and didn't get charged with the downfall of man. Yes, Lucifer, often described as the prince of evil and adversary of God, was not charged with bringing sin into the world, although we all know that Lucifer brought sin into heaven, which was the actual original sin. But God handled that debacle in heaven quite differently than he did for us here on earth—me, Adam, and the rest of humanity. God simply expelled Lucifer and one-third of the fallen angels, who stayed loyal to Lucifer from heaven, for his and their transgressions, and it is very interesting that Lucifer's original sin in heaven did not become this inherited spiritual disease or defect in angelic nature; this containment of the sin made it possible to keep heaven sin-free. One ought to speculate, Why didn't God do the same for humanity by expelling me and Adam from the earth to keep the world sin-free? After all, God chose to do this in heaven. Why not on earth? Yet God made humanity's original sin an inherited spiritual disease or defect in human nature for those humans not yet born.

Did I eat of the forbidden fruit first? Yes, yes, I did, and it was delicious, just as I'd imagined it would be, but am I guilty of bringing sin or evil into the world? Yes, I would be, but only if I were culpable, and what reasonable jury would find me guilty of or responsible for committing an evil when I didn't even know what evil was? In the prosecutor's opening statement, he quoted Aristotle. I, too, would like to quote the same quote by Aristotle, but my interpretation identifies the root cause that the prosecution negligently omitted.

Therefore, if, according to Aristotle, "the cause of a cause is the cause of that which is caused," then here is what you, the jury, must consider. God did not create the defendant with the ability to distinguish between good and evil; therefore, God caused me not to know evil. This lack of knowledge contributed to my actions of eating the forbidden fruit that caused sin to enter the world. If the trial is going to be based on Cause and Effect 101—which I agree, also, that it should be—then God should be put on trial here today and not someone who was created by a god without the ability to know good from evil. If I am without the capacity to know evil, should I be held responsible for committing evil? If God wanted a world where there would be no pain, no sickness, and no death, why would God plant this forbidden fruit right in the middle of the Garden of Eden and give to two ignorant and unaware beings both full access to it along with free will, further knowing that his (God's) greatest adversary, one with supernatural powers, was about to coax the defendant to eat of it? I failed and ate the forbidden fruit because I did not have the ability to make a wise decision, to resist it. I was created without knowledge of good and evil; I could not objectively assess the situation, for I had not the tools. I did not have comprehension and understanding; I did not have my total mind! I find it painstakingly puzzling that after God expelled Adam and me from Eden, he then thought it wise to protect the tree of life with security, as you can see in Genesis 3:24: "So he drove out the man; and he placed at the east of the garden of Eden cherubim, and a flaming sword which turned every way, to keep the way of the tree of life." This was done to keep Adam and me or any humans who would approach it from eating from the tree of life. God should have used those same angels and that burning sword to protect the tree of knowledge of good and evil from the beginning. This and several other oversights by God, not the defendant, caused sin to enter into the world. Therefore, I am not guilty.

Judge: The prosecution may call its first witness.

Prosecutor: The people call Adam.

[Bailiff takes Adam to the witness stand.]

Clerk: Please stand. Raise your right hand. Do you promise that the testimony you shall give in the case before this court shall be the truth, the whole truth, and nothing but the truth?

Adam: I do.

Clerk: Please state your first and last name.

Adam: Adam.

Clerk: And your last name, sir?

Adam: I do not have one.

Clerk: You may be seated.

Prosecutor: *[Stands up and approaches witness.]* Let's get straight to it, sir. Did you eat of the forbidden fruit, and why?

Adam: Yes, I did eat of it. The woman whom God gave to be with me, she gave me of the tree, and I did eat.

Prosecutor: *[Triumphantly smiles at Adam.]* Thank you. I have no further questions.

Judge: Does the defense have any questions?

Eve: *[Stands up.]* Yes, Your Honor. *[Approaches witness.]* Adam, why didn't you resist eating the fruit when I offered it to you?

Adam: I don't know exactly; I'm guessing for the same reason you ate of the fruit when the snake told you to. Let's face it, Eve. You and I weren't created with the greatest minds.

Eve: When God commanded of you, "But of the tree of the knowledge of good and evil, thou shalt not eat of it: for in the day that thou eatest thereof thou shalt surely die," did God explain death to you so that you understood what death actually was?

Adam: No, for I had never seen death or experienced it, for death did not exist before we ate of the fruit.

Eve: Exactly, and neither had I, for there was no death, not even in the animal kingdom, for even the animals were vegetarians. [*Eve turns to the judge.*] I would like to present as evidence Genesis 1:29–30.

Judge: You may.

Eve: Genesis 1:29–30 states, "And God said, Behold, I have given you every herb bearing seed, which is upon the face of all the earth, and every tree, in the which is the fruit of a tree yielding seed; to you it shall be for meat. And to every beast of the earth, and to every fowl of the air, and to everything that creepeth upon the earth, wherein there is life, I have given every green herb for meat: and it was so." These verses clearly reveal that man and even the carnivorous animals were to be vegetarian originally. We did not know death, so how were we to understand or fear it, Adam?

Adam: That's an excellent point.

Eve: Thank you, Adam. [*Adam and Eve gaze into each other's eyes, and one could hear a pin drop, for it is if they are reminiscing about the days of old, when they were alone in the Garden of Eden, until...*]

Prosecutor: I object, Your Honor! She's leading the witness!

Judge: Overruled! The defense may proceed.

Eve: Thank you, Your Honor. Adam, we both did not know death; therefore, we could not have understood it. Thank you. I have no further questions.

Adam: Will I ever see you again?

Eve: Only "God" knows. [*Winks.*]

Judge: Does the prosecution have any more questions for the witness?

Prosecutor: No, no, Your Honor.

Judge: The witness is excused. [*Waits for Adam to leave the stand.*] The prosecution may call the next witness.

Prosecutor: The people call Eve.

[*Bailiff takes Eve to the witness stand.*]

Clerk: Please stand. Raise your right hand. Do you promise that the testimony you shall give in the case before this court shall be the truth, the whole truth, and nothing but the truth?

Eve: I do.

Prosecutor: [*Stands up and approaches Eve.*] For six thousand years, the story has been repeated—accurately, I might add—that it was you who ate of the forbidden fruit first, then gave it to Adam. This caused the downfall of man. You just admitted to this action here today in this courtroom. How do you then claim innocence in light of your own admission of guilt for the transgression?

Eve: I stated in my opening statement that yes, I did eat of the forbidden fruit first, but I also stated that I should bear no culpability due to my ignorance.

Prosecutor: I will not allow you to waste the time of the court with games, Eve! You ate of the forbidden fruit knowing full well that you were instructed not to by God, did you not?

Eve: God never instructed me not to eat of the forbidden fruit. He instructed the man. I always wondered why he didn't communicate this important information to me. One could infer that Adam passed this information on to me. Regardless, I guess that it can be assumed that I was aware that I wasn't to eat of it.

Prosecutor: *Exactly!* You knew that you were not to eat of the forbidden fruit, yet you chose to disobey God anyway, and this comment about your "ignorance" is foolishness, for you had free will, isn't this true?

Eve: Yes, I guess one could argue that I had free will, but creating someone with free will then making that person ignorant should've been considered dangerous, one would think, under those circumstances, with the destiny of all humanity hanging in the balance.

Prosecutor: And there you have it! [*Turns to the jury.*] Of her own free will, she ate of the forbidden fruit against the orders of God!

Eve: What is so magnificent about having "free will" when you don't have your mind? [*Eve screams.*]

Prosecutor: Stop it, Eve, with this inadequate-mind thing, for you knew it was wrong to disobey God, and still, of your own free will, you failed all humanity by committing this evil act!

Eve: I was made ignorant, meaning I lacked the mental faculties needed to discern good and evil. How can it be said that I chose to disobey God truly of my own free will?

Prosecutor: You were an adult with free will, knowing right from wrong, and have admittedly confessed to disobeying God! You are guilty!

Eve: Do you have kids?

Prosecutor: Yes, yes, I do, a beautiful five-year-old daughter and a sixteen-year-old son, but what has that to do with this?

Eve: Do you have a firearm in your home?

Prosecutor: [*Turns to the judge.*] This questioning is ridiculous!

Judge: Answer the question.

Prosecutor: Yes, I have a firearm in my home for the protection of my family.

Eve: Let's say that previously you had instructed your five-year-old child never to play with the firearm because someone could be harmed or, worse, killed, yet one day, she gains access to the firearm and playfully aims it at you, pulling the trigger and mortally wounding you. Should she be charged with murder?

Prosecutor: Of course not!

Eve: She has free will, does she not?

Prosecutor: Yes, she has free will. Further, I am not a doctor and cannot speak on the intricate details of subjects such as psychology, but most of us know that generally speaking, the brain of a five-year-old is not fully developed yet!

Eve: But you told her not to play with the firearm; therefore, she was aware, and although her brain is not 100 percent developed, still, she had the capacity to know and understand what you instructed; would you not agree?

Prosecutor: Yes, but children cannot reason or control their behavior as well as adults and should, therefore, not be held to the same level of culpability! A five-year-old child would lack the capacity to understand the seriousness of what he or she had done in a situation such as this due to the lack of mental development.

Eve: You are absolutely correct. It is interesting how you can see the wrong in punishing a five-year-old child under these circumstances for murder but cannot see why I should not be held responsible for bringing sin into the world when in fact I was created with the mind of a child as it relates to understanding good and evil. A modern-day child would have perhaps fared better than I did in the Garden of Eden!

Prosecutor: [*Laughs out loud.*] Surely you are not trying to compare your mental state at the time you failed humanity to that of a five-year-old child. After all, you were a grown woman with free will and the capacity of knowing it was wrong to eat of the forbidden fruit. Please entertain the court and explain to us all why you should not be held responsible.

Eve: If free will is the power or capacity to choose among alternatives or to act in certain situations independently, be it of natural, social, or divine restraints, how could one say that I was not constrained when I did not have full mental functionality, meaning I did not have knowledge of good and evil prior to eating the fruit? And if one is to argue still that I had free will, then how can one say I intended to do wrong or evil when I did not understand what evil was? I was created not knowing evil; therefore, there was no way I could've understood the magnitude of the consequences my actions would ultimately bring about. Is it fair to charge a woman for the downfall of humanity when she did not know what evil was, a woman who was created so mentally incapacitated that she didn't even know that she was naked?

Prosecutor: [*Stumbling to respond.*] Ummm…

Eve: [*Speaks over him firmly and passionately.*] Again, by God's design, I lacked the mental ability to understand. Is it just to hold me accountable for my actions and the consequent suffering of humanity when I was created morally ignorant? Is it righteous for me to be held morally responsible for acts performed in ignorance?

Prosecutor: [*Appearing anxious, looks down at his notes.*]

Eve: Failing in the Garden of Eden was ineluctable! Don't you see? I was designed to fail! God created me ignorant of good and evil, knowing that I would be pitted against the most intelligent of all the animals created, a snake, and if you believe it was Lucifer who possessed the body of the serpent, then I was to overcome the prince of evil, the embodiment of evil, with my limited mental faculties. Is this not madness?

Prosecutor: [*Appearing exhausted, turns to the judge.*] Thank you. I have no further questions and no other witnesses, Your Honor. The people rest their case.

Eve: [*Stands up and faces the jury.*] What kind of god creates the woman, me, Eve, not whole, then expects the woman, me, Eve, to be the guardian keeping sin out of the world with the fate of all humanity hanging in the balance, yet this same god created the serpent, the wisest in the garden? Would it not have been wiser if the woman, me, Eve, had been created at least with the knowledge of good and evil?

Judge: The witness is excused. [*Waits for Eve to leave the stand.*] Is the defense ready with its case?

Eve: Yes, Your Honor. I call the serpent. [*Eve places a container that contains a king cobra in the witness chair.*]

Jury: [*Reacts with shock.*]

Judge: Order in the court!

Prosecutor: I object, Your Honor; this is blasphemy!

Judge: Overruled! The defense may proceed. [*Turns to clerk.*] No need to swear in the witness.

Clerk: Thank you, Your Honor.

Judge: [*Turns to Eve.*] You may proceed.

Eve: Thank you, Your Honor. [*Turns toward the snake.*] Well, how have you been?

Snake: Hisssssssssss ssss ss

Eve: You've gotten me into a lot of trouble since we last talked.

Snake: Hisssssssssss ssss ss

Eve: Surely you're not just going to lie there and not answer me? I, along with all the guests of the court, would love and need for you to speak today, for I am on trial for being the cause of the fall of humanity. So please tell the court how you beguiled me on the day on which I ate of the forbidden fruit.

Snake: Hissssssssssssssssssssss

Eve: [*Turns to the judge.*] Your honor, the defense requests permission to declare the witness a hostile witness. The witness is avoiding answering the questions and is refusing to speak.

Prosecutor: This is a mockery! I object, your honor!

Judge: [*Turns to prosecutor.*] Overruled! [*Turns to Eve.*] Permission is granted. The witness is declared and will be recognized by the court as a hostile witness. You may proceed.

Eve: [*Walks closer to the glass container.*] Why will you not speak? You spoke the truth in the Garden of Eden. I need you to speak truthfully again today. When I told you in the Garden of Eden if I ate from the tree of knowledge of good and evil, I would surely die, you said, "You will not die." You spoke the truth, for on that day I did not die! You also said to me, "God knows very well that the instant you eat it you will become like him, for your eyes will be opened—you will be able to distinguish good from evil!" And again, you spoke the truth, for the instant I ate of the fruit, my eyes were opened! [*Tears now run down the face of Eve, and she is now almost whispering her last question.*] Why will you not speak the truth today?

Snake: Hissssssssss ssss

Eve: I have no further questions nor witnesses. [*Returns to her chair.*]

Judge: The witness is excused. [*Waits for the bailiff to remove the snake from the witness stand.*]

Judge: Does the defense rest?

Eve: [*Stands up.*] Yes, Your Honor.

Judge: [*Turns to the jury.*] Ladies and gentlemen of the jury, I am now going to read to you the law that you must follow in deciding this case. To prove the crime charged against the defendant, the prosecution must prove three things to you: first, that the defendant ate the forbidden fruit; second, that God did not give the defendant permission to eat of the forbidden fruit; and third, that the defendant intended to bring evil or death into the world, either permanently or temporarily, sinned, and brought God's curse of death upon herself and every other living thing as well. If each of you believes that the prosecution proved all three of these things beyond a reasonable doubt, then you should find the defendant guilty. But if you believe the prosecution did not prove any one of these things beyond a reasonable doubt, then you must find the defendant not guilty. Proof beyond a reasonable doubt does not mean beyond all possible doubt. It means that you must consider all the evidence and that you are very sure that the charge is true. [*To the prosecutor and defendant.*] Are you ready with final arguments?

Prosecutor: Yes, Your Honor.

Eve: Yes, Your Honor.

Prosecutor: [*Stands up and faces the jury.*] Your Honor, and ladies and gentlemen of the jury, the judge has told you that we must prove three things. There is definitely no question about the first two criteria we must prove; after all, the defendant confesses to those. First, the defendant ate of the forbidden fruit. Second, the defendant did not have permission to eat of it. Therefore, all we have to prove is that the defendant knowingly, of her own free will, chose to disobey God and brought this evil called sin into the world, and how do we know that she knew it was wrong? Well, from her very own lips! For the defendant tells the serpent, "We may eat the fruit of the trees of the garden; but of the fruit of the tree which is in the midst of the garden, God has said, 'You shall not eat it, nor shall you touch it, lest you die.'" God never said not to touch it, but if the defendant was initially hesitating to touch it, then she knew the ramifications of eating it. The defendant wanted to be like God, knowing good and evil. Further, after committing this transgression against God, the defendant took of the fruit and gave also unto her husband, Adam, who did eat. In light of the defendant's own admissions and on the basis of the abundance of evidence, you must find the defendant guilty.

Eve: [*Stands up and faces the jury.*] Your Honor, ladies and gentlemen of the jury, I, the defendant, named Eve, was the very first woman created—well, depending on who you talk to; Lilith may have something to say about that. Regardless, I was created without the capacity of knowing good and evil, therefore not understanding either, but as the prosecutor has continually stated, I was endowed with free will. [*Eve walks closer to the jury and looks each member in the eyes.*] Jurors, can you imagine the world today if this God had created everyone as he created me in the beginning, without the knowledge of good and evil, yet giving everyone free will? Imagine that for a moment. This would be madness, would it not be? What good is free will when one does not have full capacity of the mind? I and Adam were created half-witted, or innocent, not aware of good and evil. We knew not of these things.

Simply put, I was created ignorant! Only someone lacking basic mental comprehension and understanding would eat from a tree that was said to bring death versus eating from a tree that is actually named the tree of life, that promoted immortality! [*Eve shouts passionately.*] Who chooses death over life? I'll tell you who does: someone who doesn't know what death is! I was created without this understanding and without this knowledge, yet the serpent, if it was simply a snake, was created as the most intelligent of all the creatures God made in the garden. One would think that a god would make humankind the most intelligent in the Garden of Eden, for the fate of all humanity was hanging in the balance, depending on the actions of two innocent humans who lacked knowledge of good and evil. How was I to out-think this most intelligent creature when I was designed not so intelligent? And if the snake was possessed by the devil, as many believed, then my chances of being successful at doing the right thing were even more slim, for Lucifer was a supernatural being pitted against a not-so-wise Eve. [*A tear twinkles down her face.*] After his creation of the world, God called it "good." Surely a little woman such as I and a talking snake couldn't have destroyed it all. God, being all-powerful, could have fixed my transgression and kept the world sin-free, for he did this for heaven. Is heaven still sin-free today? Lucifer sinned in heaven, yet to this day, heaven is said to still be sin-free because God wanted it to be so. If God wanted earth to be sin-free, it would be so as well.

Did I eat the forbidden fruit? Apparently, yes. Was I personally told not to eat of it? Nowhere in the Bible does it say that God told me not to eat of it. For all I knew, Adam could've been playing games with me and making fun.

Did I intentionally seek to bring evil and sin into the world? No. How can one be held responsible for intentionally causing evil, sin, pain, suffering, and death when one did not know or have an understanding of them? Also, how am I to be held responsible for doing good when I didn't understand what "good" was either? How could God's perfect creation, which he himself described ultimately as "very good," be so flawed that all it took was a talking snake and the eating of some fruit by an unclothed innocent woman and man to have it all come crashing down?

Further, and to conclude, the star witness that I called here today to testify on my behalf spoke not one word. Why is that? Was the snake suffering from fear of public speaking, or did it wish not to incriminate itself? If one of the tenets here is that you must consider all the evidence, then you all must believe beyond a reasonable doubt that on the day of the fall of humankind, a snake not only walked but talked and tricked me into eating the forbidden fruit. Does any one of you find it incredible that I am the only person to have ever lived that encountered a talking snake? If the snake never spoke, then this claim, and this trial, is a joke. The prosecution has presented no real evidence to you to show that the defendant had purposeful intent to bring evil or death into the world. The evidence does, however, clearly show that I, the defendant, committed the offense but should be found not guilty on the grounds of God inflicted ignorance. That means that there is a reasonable doubt, and, therefore, you must find the defendant not guilty.

[*Jurors are now given instructions on how to proceed and are reminded of the judge's instructions. Also, a jury foreperson is selected, and the jurors are given time see whether they can reach a verdict. After three contentious days of deliberations, of considering and debating the evidence, a verdict is finally reached.*]

Judge: Will the jury foreperson please stand? Has the jury reached a unanimous verdict?

Foreperson: Yes, Your Honor.

Clerk: The jury has determined that yes, the defendant committed the act, but due to her mental incompetence, inflicted by God himself and further compounded by the other supernatural adversary pitted against her (i.e., the talking snake), the jury finds the defendant not guilty.

Judge: [*Looks over at the jurors.*] Thank you all. You are now excused. Court is adjourned.

* * *

Note to Reader

The pretend trial of Eve is an attempt to demonstrate how she would possibly fare in an actual modern-day court of law in a civilized world that practiced fair and just hearings if she had been a real person and if it were remotely possible that the tale had actually taken place. No reasonable and fair jury today in a legitimate court of law would find Eve responsible for bringing sin into the world when considering that she was made ignorant by God —that is, she did not know good and evil and also lacked self-awareness to the degree that she didn't even know that she was naked—and further considering that she was then pitted against the supernatural forces of Lucifer and/or a talking serpent! What rational group of jurors today in a court of law and justice would hold Eve responsible for this godly debacle?

Now, turning to the secular side of this coin and examining this tale, one could argue that if we have no talking snake, we have no Adam and Eve story. Ultimately, if one is to believe that sin is a reality, then one must believe, literally and not metaphorically, the story that through the trickery of a walking, talking snake, the downfall of man was initiated. If there was never a walking, talking snake in the Garden of Eden, then the whole account is untrue. If the walking, talking snake never existed, then the Garden of Eden never existed, and if the Garden of Eden never existed, Adam and Eve never existed, and if these characters never existed, then sin in the biblical sense is unreal, and ultimately the biblical God is just as unreal as the walking, talking snake.

CHAPTER 6

God the Incompetent Creator

If the world were seeking to fill the job position titled "God," it would not be wise to select the omniscient, omnipotent and omnibenevolent biblical God, also known as Yahweh, for the position in light of his track record. But in the spirit of fairness, let's actually take a look at the résumé of the biblical deity. The Bible's claim is that God created everything and deemed it good multiple times in the book of Genesis, and even "very good" on the sixth day of creation. And if the all-knowing and all-powerful God regarded his work of creation as "very good," then how could sin spring forth in heaven, of all places, at the beginning of it all?

This should be a very troubling question for believers, for was not heaven sin-free? And if heaven was a sin-free creation, how was Satan, an angel perfectly created, capable of sinning—and sinning there? God supposedly created a completely holy heaven, the place of God's glory, sinless, with holy angels. Sin should have been impossible in heaven, the holy, glorious place of God's perfection, this place that was without sin.

Let's take an even closer look at the biblical God's "very good" creation, starting with Lucifer, often referred to as the chief among all angels, a glorious angel, one of the most honored of all angels, if not the most honored, created perfect in wisdom and beauty, a spectacle of flawlessness, who sinned in sin-free heaven. God failed to keep heaven sin-free with perfectly created angels, for Satan was not the only angel to be expelled: God had to evict one-third of his entire population of angels from heaven!

The biblical God can be called many things, but not a quitter, for after failing to keep heaven and perfectly created angels sin-free, God took his show on the road, where he created two beings less perfect or glorious than angels and without perfect wisdom, for Adam and Eve didn't even know good and evil. Their self-awareness was impaired, also, for they knew not that they were naked.

Still, God employed Adam and Eve as the gatekeepers to keep sin out of the world after knowing full well that his perfectly created angels, who possessed perfect wisdom, had previously failed to keep sin out of heaven. Not only were Adam and Eve destined to fail solely on the basis of their limited comprehension, the biblical God also allowed the same being who had sinned in heaven to orchestrate the initiation for sin on earth. And of course, ultimately Adam and Eve failed, and thus sin, causing sickness, pain, and suffering, along with death, entered the world, and the all-loving biblical God had the audacity to become angry to the point of cursing all humanity for the acts of two people who were ignorant, cursing even the ground. After God cursed all humankind with pain, sickness, and death, he then showed his loving side by making Adam and Eve coats of skins to clothe themselves with, as stated in Genesis 3:21: "Unto Adam also and to his wife did the Lord God make coats of skins, and clothed them." Then the omnibenevolent biblical God kicked them both out of Eden.

What is ironically incredible here is that after booting Adam and Eve out of the Garden of Eden for eating fruit from the tree of knowledge of good and evil, God now saw fit to station security guard angels and a flaming, whirling sword east of the Garden of Eden to guard the way to the tree of life. Fascinating how God could've done this for the tree of knowledge of good and evil while still endowing man with free will but chose not to do so. Had the security guards been placed to guard the tree of knowledge of good and evil, Adam and Eve would not have had access to it and therefore would not have been able to bring sin and death into the world, and therefore the biblical God would not have needed to punish all humanity for the acts of these two beings who did not know good and evil.

Also, are there security guard angels still guarding the tree of life in the Garden of Eden, wherever it actually is? Actually, since the Garden of Eden is on earth, shouldn't someone have come across angels, a flaming, whirling sword, and an eternal life-giving tree by now? Man has traveled to the moon and brought back moon dust, yet no living man has ever seen a leaf of this glorious tree of life. But then, Christians could argue that the entire face of the earth was completely destroyed by the biblical God when he flooded the planet for forty days and forty nights, but then the person of reason could inquire, Why didn't the biblical God have Noah place the tree of life in the ark and invite the angels who were providing security services aboard the ark so that the angels would not drown in the flood? Or did that angels die in the flood, and if so, surely the flaming, whirling sword was extinguished by the water of the flood? Maybe, just maybe, someday an archaeologist may uncover that flaming, whirling sword's remains.

But before we get into the flood story, it should be very obvious that the "very good" creation is not looking very good at this point. Let's recap what has happened thus far. First, in the beginning of the biblical God's "very good" creation, in its holiest place, called heaven, sin was committed by a supernatural, heavenly, spiritual, holy being named Lucifer, an angel. Then, in the Garden of Eden, the biblical God placed the forbidden tree of knowledge of good and evil not in a secret or guarded location or on the highest mountain in the garden; this God placed the tree of knowledge of good and evil dead center in the Garden of Eden, and he instructed two beings he'd created innocent, not knowing good and evil, to stay away from that tree, though he knew that the fate of all humanity lay in their incapable hands. If this is not incompetent, then it is surely demented.

So now let's visit the flood story with the six-hundred-year-old Noah and the ark. One would think that after the debacles of perfect angels sinning in heaven, then losing the loyalty of one-third of his angels, then even having to curse the ground after Adam and Eve failed in the Garden of Eden, the biblical God would have had easier days ahead. However, according to the Bible's chronology, just a few generations later we come across the flood story in Genesis 6:5–8 which, incredibly, states, "And God saw that the wickedness of man was great in the earth, and that every imagination of the thoughts of his heart was only evil continually. And it repented the Lord that he had made man on the earth, and it grieved him at his heart. And the Lord said, I will destroy man whom I have created from the face of the earth; both man, and beast, and the creeping thing, and the fowls of the air; for it repenteth me that I have made them. But Noah found grace in the eyes of the Lord." Throughout this writing I reference primarily the King James 1611 Bible, for it is regarded by many Christians, if not by most, to be one of the most accurate and respected Bible versions. But in this instance, I want to use a version that is more modern so that there is no misunderstanding of what is being stated here, so let's use the New American Standard Bible from 1995. In this version, Genesis 6:5–8 states, "Then the Lord saw that the wickedness of man was great on the earth, and that every intent of the thoughts of his heart was only evil continually. The Lord was sorry that He had made man on the earth, and He was grieved in His heart. The Lord said, 'I will blot out man whom I have created from the face of the land, from man to animals to creeping things and to birds of the sky; for I am sorry that I have made them.' But Noah found favor in the eyes of the Lord."

Both passages have the same meaning, of course; the latter is written in a more modern-day tongue, which should allow for easier comprehension. These biblical passages are astonishing! One should take a moment to ponder, What was humankind doing that was so wicked or evil that it moved this omnibenevolent biblical God to decide that with his omniscient mind and with his omnipotent power the only solution was the destruction of all living humans, along with every animal, bird in the sky, and insect (for the term "creeping things" means all creatures of whatever sort), sparing only Noah and his family along with two of each animal that would board the ark? This translates into killing the blind, sick, unborn, elderly, and children. Deeply contemplate the slaughter of every bird in the sky, from the hummingbird to the falcon, and every land mammal, from the majestic elephant to the bunny rabbit, yet Proverbs 12:10 states, "A righteous man regardeth the life of his beast: but the tender mercies of the wicked are cruel." If a righteous man has regard for the life of animals, then surely an all-loving, righteous God possesses this attribute as well, one would surmise. The second half of this proverb simply means that the kindest acts of the wicked are cruel, and it would appear that the God of the Bible has a tendency to demonstrate wickedness and cruelty even when he is performing kind and merciful acts, for, as if exterminating all human beings and animals wasn't enough, this compassionate, merciful God decided to kill off even the insect kingdom, eradicating everything from the butterfly to the praying mantis, yet the animals and insects had nothing to do with the wickedness of man. This is not benevolence; this is malevolence. How could the killing of bunny rabbits, kangaroos, and crickets, for example, eradicate the human wickedness and evil ways that offended the loving and merciful biblical God, or Yahweh, so? The spider that sat in its web oblivious to the acts of man had to be destroyed, too, according to the Bible, because of the acts of man.

Therefore, one must ask fervidly, What were these evil acts that warranted the killings of unborn children and innocent animals and insects? Whatever those acts were, they were horrific enough that God was sorry he had even created man, and this caused God distress! God was sorry? This is true according to the infallible word of the Bible: Genesis 6:6 reads, "And it repented the Lord that he had made man on the earth, and it grieved him at his heart." In other words, Yahweh regretted that he had made human beings on the earth, and his heart was deeply troubled. Needless to say, but how could a perfect God regret his own creation or work to the point that it made him sad, for does this not demonstrate that he acknowledges his incompetence here, or at least reveal his imperfection? And if Genesis 6:6 is incorrect, then the Bible is fallible, and therefore cannot be the word of a god, but if it is correct, then the biblical God is not God. The biblical God is said to be omniscient—he knows everything—therefore how is it possible that he is regretful and in distress when he knew in advance that he was creating flawed humans who would do wicked acts? Why is God now troubled by his creation?

And if Yahweh is regretful now because of the wickedness of humankind, if he feels now the need to destroy the world with a flood, then I say he is not only an incompetent god but a mad god as well. Yahweh, being omniscient, would have known humankind would become very wicked, for he knows everything. Yahweh, being omnipotent, created humankind to be that which he is, and if he had wanted humankind to be something other than what he is, an omnipotent God would have designed humankind to be just that. So if this god is omnibenevolent, then the God of the Bible is a lie, for an all-loving God would not, in an attempt to cleanse the earth and wash away past evils and sin, use a catastrophic flood to destroy every living human being, animal, and insect, knowing humans would just go back to being sinners afterward. This is utter madness and not the work of a compassionate and gracious deity but that of an evil and cruel one.

One can hardly imagine the devastation of life and the stench of death on earth from the decaying and rotting of countless human and animal corpses after the floodwaters subsided, but Noah could not have been faring any better on the ark, for he and his family were confined to a sealed vessel with every species of animal known on the planet in an unventilated space, surely enduring toxic conditions that would have built up from their human and animal disease-causing bacteria and the pathogens in their waste.

Apparently, the biblical deity was so grossed out by all the carnage he had caused in the world that even he was offended by it, for God promised, after Noah made an offering to him and as he received the aroma of the offering, that he wasn't ever going to use this disciplinary strategy ever again! The loving God made this promise in Genesis 8.21, "The Lord smelled the soothing aroma, and the Lord said to Himself, "I will never again curse the ground on account of man, for the intent of man's heart is evil from his youth; and I will never again destroy every living thing, as I have done."

The biblical deity also makes a promise to Noah never again to destroy the earth by flooding it, and to help himself to remember his promise, and as a sign, from that day forward he would place a rainbow in the sky after rain showers. One reads the following in Genesis 9:12–17

> God said, "This is the sign of the covenant which I am making between Me and you and every living creature that is with you, for all future generations; I have set My rainbow in the cloud, and it shall serve as a sign of a covenant between Me and the earth. It shall come about, when I make a cloud appear over the earth, that the rainbow will be seen in the cloud, and I will remember My covenant, which is between Me and you and every living creature of all flesh; and never again shall the water become a flood to destroy all flesh. When the rainbow is in the cloud, then I will look at it, to remember the everlasting covenant between God and every living creature of all flesh that is on the earth." And God said to Noah, "This is the sign of the covenant which I have established between Me and all flesh that is on the earth."

Question: Did not rainbows appear after a downpour or showers before the flood? Regardless, these passages should be cause for celebration for the believers of the faith until one comes across 2 Peter 3:10, which reads, "But the Day of the Lord will come like a thief. On that Day the heavens will disappear with a shrill noise, the heavenly bodies will burn up and be destroyed, and the earth with everything in it will vanish." Or in other words, the next time God destroys the world, it will be by fire, not by water. If God's intent for the flood was to wash away the evil and wickedness of humankind, well, the flood did not change that, for if man now has a sinful nature because of the eating of forbidden fruit by Adam and Eve, then killing everyone and especially animals and insects did not change that condition, and an omniscient deity like Yahweh would have known this, right?

Why would God pick Noah to survive the flood if he knew humans would just go back to being fallen sinners? What was the point? The flood did nothing to change humankind's sinning ways, and God admits this in Genesis 8:21, as he says, "I will never again curse the ground on account of man, for the intent of man's heart is evil from his youth; and I will never again destroy every living thing, as I have done." Astonishingly, the omniscient God says this after forty days and forty nights of flooding the earth, only to say afterward he realizes that intent of man's heart is evil from his youth. One would think that an all-knowing God would have known the heart of man prior to killing every living creature on the planet. Either the biblical God must not have known, for he did send the flood to accomplish the goal of cleansing the earth of wickedness and sin, or he did know that sending a flood would be ineffectual yet sent the flood regardless, in which case the God of the Bible is not only incompetent but profoundly immoral and evil as well. Christian apologists argue that humanity had reached a point where if God had not intervened, humankind would likely have destroyed itself. This defense of the flood by apologists then prompts the question, So in an attempt to prevent humankind from destroying itself, God decided to destroy humankind along with every other living creature on the planet as the alternative solution? The Bible claims that, like all creation, man was also created by this biblical God; is not this God then the creator of evil too?

The Greek philosopher Epicurus is accredited with asking this in the third century BCE:

> Is God willing to prevent evil, but not able? Then he is not omnipotent.

Is he able, but not willing? Then he is malevolent.

Is he both able and willing? Then whence cometh evil?

Is he neither able nor willing? Then why call him God? [32]

As Epicurus asked, if God is both able and willing to prevent evil, then why does evil exist? I would like to ask the reader again, Did God create evil? If God is the creator of all things, then surely the answer is yes. If the answer is no, then the biblical God is not the creator of all things, and he is not God. Man did not create evil, and furthermore it was committed even in heaven and committed by angels before it entered the world and then committed by lesser beings, namely humankind, according to the holy scriptures of the Bible.

Why would a supposedly omnibenevolent God create evil? The creation of evil by a supposedly omnibenevolent deity would cancel out the attribute of omnibenevolence. Christian apologists will go so far as to assert that God did not create evil but does allow evil to exist and that if God had not allowed for the possibility of evil, both humankind and angels would be serving God out of obligation, not choice. In essence God had to allow for the possibility of evil so that humankind could genuinely have free will. If this is the best defense that apologists can conjure up and is to be held as true, then the God of the Bible not only is incompetent but should be perceived as incapable; this would render him not omnipotent.

To counter the aforementioned apologists' argument, let us suppose that in order for God to allow for the possibility of sin, sin must first be in existence. Again, who created it? Continuing the counter, I propose that to say that an omniscient, omnipotent, and omnibenevolent God had to allow for the possibility of evil so that humankind could genuinely have free will is akin to saying that this all-knowing and all-powerful God had to allow for the possibility of cloudy days in order for humanity to have genuinely sunny days. After all, we are talking about God, a deity that can do anything; an omnipotent God doesn't have to bring into existence one thing in order to make

---

32   Best Quotations, "Quotes by Epicurus," January 21, 2023, https://best-quotations.com/auth-quotes.php?auth=241.

something else be. Apologists' argument that humankind's free will and not God is the creator of evil is a weak position, for when one considers that God supposedly created free will, then this makes God still the creator of evil, for if free will is the source of evil and humankind did not create free will and God did, then God created evil.

Let's turn to the Sodom and Gomorrah story to see if God fared better regarding troubles on a smaller scale, since things didn't go well on the big stages.

What was going on in the city of Sodom and Gomorrah that made the biblical deity, or Yahweh, so upset this time that he wanted to destroy these cities; what was so wicked that the Lord himself came down to earth to look into it? The logical inference is that the primary grievous sin was rampant homosexual behavior, or homosexual sex. The city's sin of sodomy became proverbial. One should not be surprised that Yahweh frowned upon homosexuality, for he clearly shares his take on the matter in Leviticus 18:22, which states, "Thou shalt not lie with mankind, as with womankind: it is abomination." And if anyone is not grasping that simple but clear passage, the Christian God lets his position again be known in the same book of Leviticus, chapter 20, verse 13, "If a man also lie with mankind, as he lieth with a woman, both of them have committed an abomination: they shall surely be put to death; their blood shall be upon them."

If one attempts to rationalize these passages as being in the Old Testament and Jehovah just being cranky, let's journey on over to the New Testament. Maybe the Lord became less harsh on the subject matter. Let's look at 1 Corinthians 6:9, "Know ye not that the unrighteous shall not inherit the kingdom of God? Be not deceived: neither fornicators, nor idolaters, nor adulterers, nor effeminate, nor abusers of themselves with mankind." The same verse translated in the International Standard Version Bible reads, "You know that wicked people will not inherit the kingdom of God, don't you? Stop deceiving yourselves! Sexually immoral people, idolaters, adulterers, male prostitutes, homosexuals." And in Romans 1:26–27 we read, "For this cause God gave them up unto vile affections: for even their women did change the natural use into that which is against nature. And likewise also the men, leaving the natural use of the woman, burned in their lust one toward another; men with men working that which is unseemly, and receiving in themselves that recompence of their error which was meet."

As one can clearly see, the deity of the Bible, Yahweh, regards homosexuality as unnatural and evil—an abomination or disgrace. Most scientists today accept that being gay is not a personal choice and that one's sexuality is predetermined and is the result of several factors, including biology and environment. If homosexuality is viewed as an abomination by the creator of all things, then why did Yahweh create this innate dimension of sexuality and then describe it with such hostile, homophobic disdain? The omnibenevolent creator created homosexuality on one hand, then took the liberty of condemning it with the other.

As one reads the story of Sodom and Gomorrah, one suddenly comes across a startling revelation regarding God's omniscience as well. Genesis 18:20–21 reads, "And the LORD said, Because the cry of Sodom and Gomorrah is great, and because their sin is very grievous; I will go down now, and see whether they have done altogether according to the cry of it, which is come unto me; and if not, I will know."

Why would God need to make a physical journey to earth to confirm information about activities that took place in Sodom and Gomorrah and to now personally visit the cities so that he may know that those acts are still being committed? God obviously did not know if the reports were true because the purpose for the earthly visit was to verify by visiting Sodom and Gomorrah so that he could see and confirm the wickedness before destroying the cities. The passages of Genesis 18:20–21 contradict the powers of the supposed omniscient deity, who is said also to be omnipresent. If Yahweh knows everything and is everywhere at the same time, then why would this god need to travel some place he should already be in existence at and then need to find out that which he should already have knowledge of?

As if the Lord's having to hear many times that the people of Sodom and Gomorrah were very evil and having to go and see whether the people were as bad as he had heard in order for him to know for sure weren't astonishing enough for a god who is supposed all-knowing and is everywhere at the same time, then the biblical deity's bargaining with Abraham for the lives of any righteous people who might be living in Sodom and Gomorrah is even more startling! In Genesis 18:23–33, Abraham bargains with and asks God, Will he destroy the good people while he is destroying the evil as well? God's response to the number given by Abraham is that if he should discover that number of righteous given to him, he will not destroy the city. Wait—God says *if* he finds? Shouldn't God know how many righteous people are already living in Sodom?

Genesis 18:23–33 reads like this:

> And Abraham drew near, and said, Wilt thou also destroy the righteous with the wicked? Peradventure there be fifty righteous within the city: wilt thou also destroy and not spare the place for the fifty righteous that are therein? That be far from thee to do after this manner, to slay the righteous with the wicked: and that the righteous should be as the wicked, that be far from thee: Shall not the Judge of all the earth do right? And the Lord said, If I find in Sodom fifty righteous within the city, then I will spare all the place for their sakes. And Abraham answered and said, Behold now, I have taken upon me to speak unto the Lord, which am but dust and ashes: Peradventure there shall lack five of the fifty righteous: wilt thou destroy all the city for lack of five? And he said, If I find there forty and five, I will not destroy it. And he spake unto him yet again, and said, Peradventure there shall be forty found there. And he said, I will not do it for forty's sake. And he said unto him, Oh let not the Lord be angry, and I will speak: Peradventure there shall thirty be found there. And he said, I will not do

it, if I find thirty there. And he said, Behold now, I have taken upon me to speak unto the Lord: Peradventure there shall be twenty found there. And he said, I will not destroy it for twenty's sake. And he said, Oh let not the Lord be angry, and I will speak yet but this once: Peradventure ten shall be found there. And he said, I will not destroy it for ten's sake. And the Lord went his way, as soon as he had left communing with Abraham: and Abraham returned unto his place.

According to the scriptures, the sin of sodomy was a very grievous offense, and this rampant homosexual behavior reached the home of Lot when every man in the town came to his home to gang-rape the two male angels who had accompanied God earlier in the day. The International Standard Version of Genesis 19:4–11 reads like this:

Before they could lie down, all the men of Sodom and its outskirts, both young and old, surrounded the house. They called out to Lot and asked, "Where are the men who came to visit you tonight? Bring them out to us so we can have sex with them!" Lot went outside to them, shut the door behind him, and said, "I urge you, my brothers, don't do such a wicked thing. Look here, I have two daughters who are virgins. Let me bring them out to you, and you may do to them whatever you wish, only don't do anything to these men, because they're here under my protection." But they replied, "Get out of the way! This man came here as a foreigner, and now he's acting like a judge! So, we're going to deal more harshly with you than with them." Then they pushed hard against the man (that is, against Lot), intending to break down the door. But the angels inside reached out, dragged Lot back into the house with them, shut the door, and blinded the men who were at the entrance of the house, from the least important to the greatest, so they were unable to find the doorway.

It is incredible to note here that Lot, the supposed only righteous man in the city, offered up his two virgin daughters to be gang-raped by the mob. What a horrific and indefensible gesture suggested by Lot, and Yahweh was silent. Eventually Sodom was destroyed by God primarily because of homosexuality. Surely, there had to have been children and perhaps pregnant women carrying their unborn. Surely, they were not evil. Or was Sodom 100 percent homosexual, and if Sodom was 100 percent homosexual, how was the city repopulating itself?

As stated earlier in this chapter, some Christian apologists argue that God did not create evil. It's amazing that they argue this when it clearly states in scriptures like Isaiah 45:7, "I form the light, and create darkness: I make peace, and create evil: I the Lord do all these things." Also, Lamentations 3:38 reads, "Out of the mouth of the most High proceedeth not evil and good?" And 1 Samuel 18:10 reads, "And it came to pass on the morrow, that the evil spirit from God came upon Saul, and he prophesied in the midst of the house: and David played with his hand, as at other times: and there was a javelin in Saul's hand." These passages show not only that the biblical deity peddles in evil but that he is its creator as well. Apologists desperately embrace the free will excuse card to give the biblical God a way out from being held accountable for creating evil, but if Yahweh is all-powerful, it would be possible for this deity to create free will and not be obligated to create evil. After all, this is the same God that made an ass talk, is it not?

It would seem a bit disingenuous for God to call something good when he knew that he had also created evil. The Bible stories mentioned within this chapter reveal a god who is either incompetent, not omnipotent, or simply a myth. For where is the reasonableness in asserting that an omnipotent God created the creation, yet an innocent and completely ignorant woman and man, by simply eating fruit, corrupted it all? This would be utter nonsense, for only God would be capable of corrupting and destroying that creation, not two naked humans who knew not what corruption was!

According to apologists, nothing is ever the biblical God's fault, but this, too, is utter nonsense. Lucifer sinned in the very beginning of time in heaven because of pride. Who created Lucifer with that pride? Yahweh. It defies basic logic that God would create evil, and when humankind dabbled in evil God, decided to flood the earth. If humankind is the creation of God, then whatever humankind is, that's what humankind was created as by God. Humanity cannot alter that, just as the moon cannot ever become the sun. Humankind cannot ever become something other than what humankind was created as, and if God isn't pleased with the design, then he, being omnipotent, should have chosen another design.

In the small sample of stories I've addressed in this chapter, there is one common denominator, from the fall of angels in heaven at the very beginning of time to the destruction of Sodom and Gomorrah: things went wrong when God was supposed to have made everything "good." If the God of the Bible were truly omnipotent, then angels would not have failed in heaven, sin would not have entered the Garden of Eden, there wouldn't have been a need to flood and kill everything on the planet, and there would not have been a need to destroy cities because they became evil when God had made mankind evil. The biblical God's plans in the Bible stories always fail, according to his own holy scriptures. Given that the common denominator is the biblical God, one could surmise that if the biblical God were indeed a reality, the fault would lie with him and not the creations brought forth by him.

CHAPTER 7
Biblical Infallibility

That which brought forth the cosmos and dressed it in all its magnificence and celestial splendor, setting into motion the rising and setting of the earth's sun and moon; that which brought forth the song of the nightingale and powerful roar of the earth's ocean waves; that which brought into existence the petals of the flower and the talons of the eagle, and that which brought forth all manner of life and human consciousness and awareness of this reality called life is not that which would have need of inspiring authorship for the writings of a puny book named the Bible by the creation called man and then charging fallible man with bringing it into existence, infallible. That which brought forth creation requires not love, nor belief, nor worship by humanity. The writings of that which brought forth creation are the pebbles that the common ant can lift with its mandibles to the pebbles we call asteroids, which can be hundreds of miles long and which revolve around planet Earth's sun.

That which brought forth creation, such as the human brain and the complexity of the human brain and mind, which are capable of functions such as, but not limited to, dreaming, awareness, memory, thought, emotion, and vision, needs not the hand of man to pen its writings. Interestingly, one can physically touch the brain, but the mind is untouchable. The mind is intangible and, much like the universe, possibly limitless. This is how that which brought forth all creation authors; it would not need the assistance of man to prove to man that it, she, or he is a reality. And if that which brought into creation all that there is in existence desired a relationship or the realization of itself, herself, or himself by humanity or desired love, desired belief, or desired worship, then humanity would come to know of this desire by way of a natural phenomenon and not by way of a man-made written book that invites humanity into a game of hide-and-seek, confusion, and mental suffering, for no man has ever seen the biblical God, or any other deity from any other religious text for that matter.

That the creator of such a magnificent world would require blind belief is puzzling when one considers certain attributes bestowed upon humankind, those being intellect and reason, yet one is to believe that the biblical God is real and that in order to realize and connect with the biblical God one must blindly trust in a book and simply believe, and this will make the Christian God happy. Humankind, being made creatures of intellect and reason, might ponder why a god would then require human beings to realize him only through blind faith as opposed to reason and intellect.

Without error, that which brought forth creation brought into existence every celestial body and particle of the universe, every bird of the sky, every fish of the sea, every mammal on planet Earth; every flower and every tree, every insect, everything seen and everything that is incapable of being seen or known by humankind has been created without error, including the creation called humankind.

I surmise, contradictory to the Bible, that humankind is also created without error. Only religious man-written books declare that humanity is flawed, not nature. That source or power that brought the world into existence caused it to be so magnificently; therefore, would not the message to humanity from that which brought all into existence be communicated in a natural, magnificent manner as well? That which created such a magnificent world would have also created a natural, magnificent communication method, undoubtedly.

Yet men of past generations have handed down for centuries a collection of religious texts now called the Bible—purportedly the word of God, say the words of man within this book, without any evidence or confirmed, reliable witnesses to a supernatural origin of these religious texts, yet one is to simply believe that the Bible is of divine origin. Humankind cannot create the sun, nor can we manipulate the rising or setting of it; man cannot create a planet such as Earth or that which holds it in orbit as it rotates the sun; man cannot even create one drop of natural rain or that natural cloud from which natural rain falls, but humans can write a book and within those writings create a god, and men have created many. And with the man-made holy book called the Bible, man has had the power to modify, revise, deny access to, burn, banish, misinterpret, conceal, add to, or subtract from it, or, in other words, manipulate this book of paper and ink called the Bible.

How can anything so important to humanity and supposedly inspired by God be so exploited and controlled by man? The Bible does not share the same degree of preeminence as the sun, the moon, or any celestial creation; nor does it embody magnificence like the redwood tree or the common housefly. These are creations of magnificence; therefore, would not the word of God be a natural magnificent phenomenon as well?

The Bible's writings are claimed to be "God-breathed," yet the Bible lacks the characteristics and qualities of that handiwork which brought forth this existence. It lacks the artistry; it lacks the craftsmanship of all the other natural creations, for how can the Bible be a special, inspired creation from a god when men of power can make its teachings illegal to practice? How is it divine, when man can add to and subtract from it—and has added to and subtracted from it—to make changes to it? The word of God would never be in the form of a book that can have and has had writings go missing only to be discovered in caves and under rocks hundreds of years after their supposed inspiration. Could one imagine the sun going missing for a few minutes? Could one imagine man attempting to outlaw the sunshine? The

Bible cannot be of the same author who wrote the stars into the night skies, nor can the Bible's claimed God be the same maker that brought forth the metamorphosis of the caterpillar into the butterfly.

According to the Bible, in the beginning God created the sun on the fourth day. This would mean that every human born would receive and enjoy its light and warmth. One has to ponder why Yahweh would take up to approximately 1,500 years to inspire the completion of his biblical texts—this while taking off a few hundred years during the period known as the "four hundred silent years," or, officially, the intertestamental period. One would think that if this biblical God's message were so important and the Old Testament deity Yahweh desired every human to receive his word, it, too, would have been created in the very beginning directly from him, without error, just like the light of the sun. Christians would have one believe that this God created the sun, which is the light of the world, instantly in one singular day but "inspired" the creation of his word, the Bible, which is regarded as the light of humanity, in approximately 1,500 years! The idea of the deity of the Christian Bible being the author of creation causes much reasonable doubt and suspicion, for the objective fact is that many men wrote the Bible over a very long period.

The Bible claims that God created the world in six days and called it good, meaning that he was finished, as I've stated previously in this writing, yet it is general knowledge that at this very moment the universe is still creating itself with its continued present expansion, with new worlds, stars, planets, moons, galaxies, and quite possibly life—and even intelligent life—coming into creation extraordinarily. Just as these creations are being born today and at this very moment without Yahweh being the orchestrator, so it was at the beginning of time and the creation of the world.

Again, the deity of the Christian Bible cannot be the author of creation if the Bible is the only proof, for the Bible was written by man, and the God of the Bible, like all the gods that preceded Yahweh, sprang from man's imagination. There is absolutely nothing about the Bible that identifies it as divine, absolutely nothing about it that makes it special to anyone outside those willing to believe the claims within it, which man wrote. A god would not create humankind to be the most intelligent creature on this planet, in this solar system, and in this galaxy yet require this same intelligent being to become very unintelligent by believing that a talking snake somehow tricked humanity into committing an act that made humanity evil and the world corrupt. God's claimed message, the Bible, should embrace humanity's intellect, not insult it.

How is one to simply have belief in a story describing a god as all-powerful and all-knowing, desiring to create the world, which he then does and calls it good, only to have a talking snake trick a woman into eating a forbidden fruit to corrupt it all? This does not sound like the work of an all-powerful god but like a man-made story, an attempt to explain the conditions of the world as it was. One is asked to believe that the same biblical deity who punished all humanity for the acts of two people, Adam and Eve, who, in the book of Genesis, were tasked with only one responsibility and failed, would still later choose man to bring the Bible into the world, which that deity would inspire at his leisure for a span of approximately 1,500 years, using multiple writers and expecting the finished product to be, well, inerrant?

Theologians and apologists claim the Bible to be inerrant and infallible, yet it is anything but these. How can anyone claim that the Bible is infallible or inerrant when the very first book of Genesis contains two creation stories that contradict each other? If the Bible disagrees with itself, then it can be neither reliable nor the work of a god. Nothing in creation, nothing that came into being, contradicts itself so grossly as the biblical text.

I wish not to speak in absolutes, for there are occasional aberrations in nature from time to time, but to the point, the sun is never the moon, and the moon is never planet Mars. The falcon never roars, and the lion never takes flight to soar above in the sky. Simply put, creation doesn't contradict itself, for creation is inerrant, yet the biblical texts, or supposed inspired word of God, are not. How was Yahweh able to create everything in creation inerrant but unable to create his "inspired" word, the Bible, inerrant?

The biblical text is inconsistent with all other creations brought forth by that which brought forth creation. Intelligently, one could infer that the author of the world is not the author of the book called the Bible. The Bible claims that Yahweh is the creator of all that there is, and if this were in fact true, then Yahweh would've done a magnificent job. But how is humanity to believe that Yahweh is the same God who created the wings of the butterfly but is also the author and creator of a book that is contradictory and discrepant, approves of outrageous injustice and cruelty, contains false prophecies, and is written by unknown authors?

Further, devoted Christians can't even agree on the teachings, practices, and interpretations consistently. Nor can their church leaders, for Baptists, Lutherans, Methodists, Presbyterians, Jehovah's Witnesses, Mormons, and Roman Catholics, just to list a few, interpret, teach, and practice the biblical scriptures differently. One would think that if it were true that the biblical God "inspired" the writings of the Bible, then this same deity would "inspire" man with the ability to comprehend it as well. Every man, woman, and child should be able to read the Bible and receive the exact same comprehension and understanding of it. There would not be any misinterpretation or lack of comprehension from any reader if the Bible were truly the word of God. One would not and should not need a master's degree in theology to understand a supposed communication sent from God to humanity.

Men of power and influence in the church for approximately two thousand years have twisted the Bible to their own liking—thus the numerous denominations, which currently number over forty thousand worldwide! If there were truly a God and that God were the creator of this world and the designer of the wings of the butterfly, then if that God desired to communicate a message to mankind, that word or message would be a thing of beauty, like the transformation of the caterpillar into the butterfly. The metamorphosis of the caterpillar into the butterfly never contradicts itself; the caterpillar never becomes a blue whale. Should not the word of God be noncontradictory as well? And if any book claimed to be the word of God holds but one contradiction, it cannot and should not be regarded as the work of the creator of the world or that of a god.

The count of the exact number of contradictions varies, depending on which source one holds as more credible than the others, but whatever the count, it is far too many, for if the biblical God had brought forth all things in creation perfectly, Yahweh would have been powerful enough to ensure that his 1,500-years-in-the-making "inspired" word, the Bible, would have been brought forth without error, like everything else he is credited with creating. Apologists and believers rarely admit to the errors; when they do, to explain away the errors, they will, of course, argue that the Bible is, yes, inspired by God, but man penned it; then the quick, intelligent, and logical response should be that this is exactly why an all-knowing God would not have utilized man to perform the task, and certainly not for a span of approximately 1,500 years!

I am a man of flesh and blood and most certainly not the creator of time, space, or matter, and to top it off, I'm not even all-knowing, but I am smart enough to not dictate to over forty different writers for even one year at different times of that year in the hopes that all these writers will finally compile a manual for something important and emergent to be produced without error at the end of that one year. Therefore, only a trickster would attempt to convince one that an all-powerful and all-knowing God would, and for a period of 1,500 years!

Previously in this writing, I stated that the word of God would have been created like the light and warmth of the sun, readily available for all humankind to receive it on day one of creation and not made available, like the Bible, over one thousand five hundred years later. Genesis 2: says, "And the LORD God formed man of the dust of the ground, and breathed into his nostrils the breath of life; and man became a living soul." Here Yahweh is said to have created a whole adult man instantly! Researchers have calculated that there are

37.2 trillion cells in the human body, yet this wasn't even a day's work for Yahweh. Yahweh molded Adam from some dirt from the ground and breathed into his nostrils, and those 37.2 trillion cells in his human body sprang to life, and Adam became a living, error-free being. Hallelujah! And to reemphasize: after Yahweh created, without error, without contradiction, simply by speaking it into existence instantaneously, that ball of fire, that star, our sun, which sits at the center of our solar system, and after he created Adam by simply molding him from the dust of the ground, still, his word, the Bible, took generations to come off the press, and yet it contains numerous errors and contradictions! Surely and without a doubt, that which authored the creation of the sun and humankind is not the author of the Bible. This claim is an insult to all creation and to the reasonable mind.

Further, we are now in the year 2023, and one would think that after 1,500 years of Yahweh "inspiring" his message, coupled with the canonization of it, and then approximately 2,000 additional years elapsing after Christ, all people of the earth would have received his message by now and would have heard of this divine word, but shockingly, no. Some Christian missionary groups estimate that over a billion people in the world today have little to no knowledge of Yahweh, of Jesus, or of the Gospels, and more astonishingly, there's very little chance of them hearing the aforementioned before they die. How is this possible? In the year 2023, there are remote populations completely cut off from the knowledge of the Christian faith. These groups have no known believers, no Bible translated into their language, and no Christian churches erected in their societies. Further, currently there are no Christian missionary groups even trying to reach them! For approximately two thousand years, these people have been born and died, and they will continue to be born and will continue to die in these societies without ever having an opportunity to hear about or read the Bible, this supposed divine word of God.

How is it possible that this supposed divine word of God has yet to reach all the people of the world because of obstacles, yet the sun finds its way to them every day in spite of those obstacles? This fact alone is astonishing evidence that the Bible cannot have been authored by the author that authored the creation of the world. That which brought forth creation would not be dependent on man having the ability to reach these remote populations. That which brought forth the world did not wait 1,500 years to give the flower sunlight or 1,500 years to give the fish water; nor would the creator of the world wait 1,500 years to give humanity word via a book to realize its, his, or her existence—and depending on how remote your village was, you might not receive the word at all. Billions of people have been born and have died, and many more will be born and they, too, will die, without ever knowing of Christianity, Yahweh, or Jesus Christ, further demonstrating that the Bible is incompatible with all other creations deemed to be the work of a god and cannot be the work of that which brought forth this existence.

Imagine the creator of life needing man to deliver his word by horse and buggy, boat, car, or airplane. The light of the sun has been delivered to every human that ever walked the earth, from *Homo habilis* to us, modern-day man, *Homo sapiens*. If the creator of this world had a message for humanity, that message would have been received by all humanity from the beginning of time to today. And all human beings would receive this message, like the warmth of the sun, for themselves and would need not an intermediary or translator to understand that word or message. The creator or a god would not still be attempting to reach people in remote, isolated areas of the world because the Christian missionaries cannot make it to these very difficult-to-reach locations of the world in 2023! To simply summarize the point here, I will reiterate that one must inquire as to how it is that the supposed biblical deity can have delivered sunshine, rain, and oxygen to all humanity and all living things since the genesis of time yet cannot deliver his "inspired" word with the same competence.

Man wrote the Bible and created Yahweh, Jesus Christ, Lucifer, Adam and Eve, and the talking snake. These characters must be man-made constructs, for all these stories are fables that are superstitious, unnatural, and inaccurate on all secular levels as they pertain to scientific explanations of how creation came to be. Yet that which brought forth life, from the seemingly limitless human mind to the seemingly limitless expansion of the cosmos, brought forth creations that are without error. These are not the works of man but are of that which brought forth all there is, and that creator concerns itself not with the matters of the ant, the lion, the fish of the sea, or the birds of the sky or those regarding humanity. That which brought forth creation does not produce such faulty, erroneous works as the Bible, and if there were a male God sitting up in the sky, observing the assertion that this was his work, I'm sure he would reveal himself out of embarrassment under these conditions, just to make it clear that he had nothing to do with the folly called the Bible, and would say in a thunderous voice so that all humankind would hear, "I am not affiliated in any way with this work called the Bible!" The word of the creator of the world would not have come to the Native Americans of North America through the agencies of brutality and genocide at the hands of their Christian European conquerors, nor to today's African Americans through the agencies of slavery, rape, lynching, dehumanization, torture, and mass murder, better known as the transatlantic slave trade, just to name two historical atrocities that brought Christianity to the ancestors of today's Native Americans and African Americans. An all-loving God would not dispatch his word in this manner through the means of slavery, rape, torture, and murder.

Here, I have listed two alarming issues with the word of God, the Bible, one being human inability to deliver this message to all the people in the world and the second being the horrific ways this message has historically been delivered to Native Americans and African Americans. These are but two, for there have been many crusades and conquests drenched in blood in the attempt to convert and Christianize by spreading the teachings of the Bible or the word of God. The Bible is errant and fallible, and these qualities render the Bible unqualified to be the work of that which brought forth all creation.

CHAPTER 8

Soulless Man

And the Lord God formed man of the dust of the ground, and breathed
into his nostrils the breath of life; and man became a living soul.
—*Genesis 2:7*

A book made of paper inked with the writings by unknowledgeable men of the time in their attempt to add context to the reality of their existence and that of all living things in the creation of life says that a god that does not exist created something that more than likely, too, does not exist: the soul. For what is the soul, and isn't it strange that in 2023 man is still seeking to find it, although supposedly it is within every human and, some claim, every animal?

Since the dawn of the human race, billions of people have lived and billions have died, yet not one soul has ever been identified in any human body. If humankind possesses this soul and it is what makes us *us*, and if it is immortal, should we not know of it?

The Christian religion requires one to believe in a god that one has never seen, a god that is outside time, matter, and space; this god is said to be outside that which humanity inhabits, but the soul is said to inhabit every living being, though just like God, it, too, has never been realized by any human being or animal, ever. The soul is believed to be the immaterial part of a human being or animal and is

regarded as immortal. If this is factual, where is the medical confirmation or scientific proof? Or, just as with God, is realization of the
soul's existence dependent on religious belief? The soul, after all, too, is
a religious concept and not a proved or discovered biological reality. It,
too, is a construct of philosophical and mythological traditions; currently, no scientific evidence whatsoever supports the existence of the
immortal soul. Scientists are currently closer to determining whether
certain types of mushrooms can actually talk to one another by sending electrical signals through their hyphae and whether they may have
a vocabulary of about fifty words than they are to capturing a human
immortal soul in a jar.

Christians were introduced to the soul in the same way they were
introduced to Yahweh: through the religious text called the Bible.
Therefore, Christianity presupposes, the soul has to be a real thing because it's in the Bible. The Hebrew word *nephesh*, which was originally
used to mean "throat" but was then used to refer to the whole person
or animal, is now translated as "soul." This English word gives it the
meaning of an immortal, spiritual, or immaterial part of a human
being or animal.

In the original Hebrew texts, in the book of Genesis, both humans and animals were called "living *nephesh*." In the original Hebrew
Bible, the word *nephesh* actually meant a living, breathing physical
being, either man or animal. The original languages in which the Bible
was written include ancient Hebrew, which was the tongue of the ancient Israelites and the language in which most of the Old Testament
was penned. A few of the original passages in the Old Testament were
written in Aramaic, and the original New Testament is said to have
been written totally in Greek.

To be more concise, the original ancient biblical texts written in
Hebrew used the word *nephesh*, and its meaning was simply "a living
being" when it was read in its proper context in Genesis 2:7 and thus
we have the translation "And the Lord God formed man of the dust of
the ground, and breathed into his nostrils the breath of life; and man

became a living soul." This verse does not say anything about an immortal soul being placed into man; it says only that he, Adam, is one. In the original Hebrew texts, the immortal-soul concept was never mentioned; the word *nephesh* was used some 754 times, and, again, not once was it used in reference to an immortal spiritual or immaterial part of a human being or animal but instead denoted a living being, be it man, animal, or perhaps even the biblical God Yahweh himself!

Leviticus 26:11 reads, "And I set my tabernacle among you: and my soul shall not abhor you." Here one could infer that the biblical God, Yahweh, who is said to be a spirit, possesses a soul. Interesting. For Christians who subscribe to the belief that humans have souls, which is how they will be transported into the next life, for the soul is immortal, then how can this assertion be true if in the book of Ezekiel there are passages that speak of the death of the soul? Ezekiel 18:4 reads, "Behold, all souls are mine; as the soul of the father, so also the soul of the son is mine: the soul that sinneth, it shall die." And Ezekiel 18:20 reads, "The soul that sinneth, it shall die." Also in this Old Testament book of Ezekiel, chapters and verses further demonstrate that the word *nephesh*, translated here with the word *soul*, is not connected with immortality, for again these passages speak of the death of the soul.

If one were to translate Ezekiel 18:4 more accurately, it would read, "Behold, all living beings are mine; as the being of the father, so also the being of the son is mine: the being that sinneth, it shall die." The English word *soul* has its roots in ancient Greek philosophy, which held the belief in an immaterial, immortal part of all humans, but this belief was not that of the ancient Hebrew writers of the biblical texts, for again, *nephesh* meant a living being.

It cannot be overstated that *nephesh* did not then and does not now mean the immaterial part of a human being or animal, regarded as immortal, and that the immortality concept was totally foreign to the original Hebrew Bible. Those who would still argue that all beings have immortal souls must explain how the soul is not immortal in their holy book, the Bible, in scriptures such as Ezekiel 18:4 and Ezekiel 18:20. Over seven hundred times, the ancient Hebrew word *nephesh* appears in the original ancient Hebrew Bible, and if *nephesh* has now been replaced with the English word *soul* over seven hundred times, this means that the immortality concept has been embraced incorrectly for the word *nephesh*.

The biblical texts promise believers eternal life, and it is understood that the physical body does not survive physical death. From reading the Bible correctly, we know that the word *soul* replaced the original ancient Hebrew word *nephesh*, rendering the immortal-soul concept void. The theological belief that humankind has three parts, also known as trichotomy, asserts that humankind is body, soul, and spirit. The physical vehicle, the body, and two immaterial parts, the soul—which is believed to be the essence of the being, or that which makes one who one is, that is, personality, mind, will, emotions, and so on—and finally the spirit, which is believed to be that immaterial part that connects man with God. Unlike with the immaterial, immortal soul that is said to be a part of all humans, it is believed by Christians that only believers are spiritually alive and that nonbelievers are spiritually dead. Thus, in order to have the ability to have a relationship with God, one must be a believer, and once this hurdle is cleared, one is then anointed spiritually alive.

To be clear, in the Bible, at times it appears that the words *spirit* and *soul* are the same and that the words are used interchangeably, but within New Testament scriptures such as Hebrews 4:12 the two are clearly distinguished: "For the word of God is quick, and powerful, and sharper than any two-edged sword, piercing even to the dividing asunder of soul and spirit, and of the joints and marrow, and is a discerner of the thoughts and intents of the heart." But here, when one knows how to read the word *soul* correctly, one could argue that this verse could also read, "For the word of God is quick, and powerful, and sharper than any two-edged sword, piercing even to the dividing asunder of being and spirit, and of the joints and marrow, and is a discerner of the thoughts and intents of the heart." Interesting!

1 Thessalonians 5:23 distinguishes the word *soul* from being and *spirit* from soul. It reads, "And the very God of peace sanctify you wholly; and I pray God your whole spirit and soul and body be preserved blameless unto the coming of our Lord Jesus Christ." So which immortal, immaterial part of humanity goes to heaven, the spirit or the soul? We all know that it's not the physical body, and we should know now that the immortal-soul concept is void because of the misinterpretation of the word *nephesh*, for again, *nephesh*'s original meaning was not that of immortality, which leaves only the spirit. The spirit is the only vehicle left to grant immortality, for it cannot be the body nor the soul.

Further, the Bible identifies the spirit as that vehicle in Ecclesiastes 12:7, which states, "Then shall the dust return to the earth as it was: and the spirit shall return unto God who gave it." Please note that the soul was not mentioned here, and if the soul were immortal, would not Yahweh mention it here?

So let's investigate the spirit. Now, if only believers in Jesus Christ are spiritually alive and nonbelievers are spiritually dead, does this mean that the nonbelievers are without a spirit in their bodies or in their minds? If the spirit is a real part of the human body and that body is alive, how can it possess something that is dead? To use the Christian vernacular, the Christian faith's position is that we are all born spiritually dead because of the fall of man in the Garden of Eden and that to become spiritually alive, one must come to Jesus through faith or, as it reads in Romans 10:9 "That if thou shalt confess with thy mouth the Lord Jesus, and shalt believe in thine heart that God hath raised him from the dead, thou shalt be saved." Or in other words, one's belief in Jesus renders one spiritually alive, for "spiritually dead" is believed to mean one is separated from the Christian God, Jesus Christ.

In the attempt to comprehend this spiritual phenomenon, the spirit that is claimed to be a real part of every living being, the reasonable and sound minded among the living struggle with the assertion that all beings are born with a part that is dead within because of a talking, walking snake tricking an unclothed woman into eating a fruit, a woman who caused her man also to eat of it in the beginning of creation, causing the so-called immaterial, spiritual part of all beings to be dead upon arrival at birth, but incredibly, that individual's spirit part is activated and brought to life when a particular deity is verbally acknowledged to be real, and that being must now also believe with his or her heart that the deity Jesus Christ was crucified on a cross and that this god-man rose from the dead. This renders a being's spirit alive!

Respectfully, I must ask, How can any reasonably intelligent being hold this as truth? In short, in order to have one's immaterial, immortal spirit part functioning properly or to be spiritually alive, one must be a Christian or believer that Jesus is the Christ. This is absolutely incredible! This would mean, if it were true, that nonbelievers and other peoples of the world who subscribe to other gods and religions are spiritually dead. The Muslims believe Jesus was a prophet; are the Muslims spiritually dead? The Hindus have millions of gods; not one of them is named Jesus Christ; are the Hindus spiritually dead? And what about the Jews? It is written in the Bible—by the Jews themselves, I might add—that they are the chosen people of Yahweh. Deuteronomy 14:2 reads, "For thou art a holy people unto the Lord thy God, and the Lord hath chosen thee to be a peculiar people unto himself, above all the nations that are upon the earth." The Jews, however, do not believe that Jesus was the Messiah or the Christ! Are the Jews, too, spiritually dead?

Further, I would be remiss if I didn't speak more on the fact that the Jews do not believe that Jesus was or is the prophesied Christ or Messiah. The Jews are the authors of the Old Testament and creators of Yahweh, who is claimed to be the father of Jesus, the Messiah. If the Jews do not accept the Jesus Christ story, who are the non-Jews to argue with the Jews about the authenticity of Jesus Christ being the son of God and the Messiah or their rejection of that idea? At this point, it's not looking good for humanity having eternal life, be it in hell or heaven, for there is no vehicle for transport to that afterlife. The body dies here on earth. The soul is basically a new concept versus the original concept and meaning of *nephesh*, and the spirit is viable only if one accepts and believes that a real live talking snake tricked a woman into eating forbidden fruit, which corrupted humanity's spirit, but a guy named Jesus fixed it all by getting crucified and rising from the dead—but not believing in this incredible account renders that part of you, the spirit, dead.

Where does this leave humanity in the hopes of immortality? What is this inside us, then, if humanity does not have a soul or spirit? It's called the brain. One must understand that the spirit and the soul are religious concepts. That is why neither can be found, along with God. There is no scientific evidence whatsoever to support the existence of the soul, the spirit, or God.

So, again, all that remains is the brain. And inside the physical brain lies the intangible mind, and from the mind of man, in his desire to understand and make sense of the world and the desire for immortality, sprang beliefs in the immortal spirit and God. There is no supernatural soul or supernatural spirit, only the human mind housed in the complex organ called the brain. And interestingly enough, the mind can be said to be immaterial, yet without the physical brain, there is no mind, for once the physical body dies, so goes the mind; sadly, nothing physical survives physical death.

One could argue, and justifiably so, that if humanity can have a real, immaterial mind, why not a real, immaterial soul and spirit? And a reasonable response could be that every day we human beings experience this mind inside ourselves. Well, maybe I shouldn't say all of us, but many of us experience thinking, imagination, emotions, reasoning, and decision-making. These incredible functions prove that there is something going on inside most of our heads. I challenge any apologist of Christianity to deliver evidence for the reality of the immortal soul or the supernatural spirit.

The speculation, hope, or religious belief in the immortal soul and supernatural spirit does not make them a reality; these concepts sprang from the mind of man. Further, the concept of soul and spirit, as they pertain to religion, comes from books of belief, not books of scientific facts. It is often said that what the heart wants, the mind will create. For Christians, their belief in the immortal soul and spirit comes from their religious text, the Bible, which also teaches them of a man parting a sea with a staff and of a man named Balaam having a full-blown conversation with his talking ass. What are the chances that these accounts really happened? I would surmise that the chances of those accounts being true are about the same as the chances of humanity having an immortal soul.

CHAPTER 9

No Resurrection, No Rapture

*And if Christ be not risen, then is our preaching
vain, and your faith is also vain.*
—1 Corinthians 15:14

1 Corinthians 15:14 is perhaps the most powerful verse in all the New Testament, for if there was not a man who, as it is claimed, was a miracle worker and the son of God who rose from the dead, then the faith known as Christianity is, simply and undisputedly, fictitious. Further, if a man named Jesus did not rise from the dead, then, too, the fall-of-man story of the talking snake tempting the woman and that woman giving the man the forbidden fruit that supposedly brought a condition called sin into the world is untrue, for the sole purpose of the crucifixion is that the biblical God sent his only begotten son, Jesus, into the world in order that the world might be saved through him. By sacrificing himself on a cross for all humanity, Jesus supposedly died for all humanity's sins at once. But again, if Jesus never rose from the dead, then the Jesus Christ resurrection story is undisputedly the greatest falsehood known to modern man.

Who makes this claim that a man named Jesus was crucified and rose from the darkness of death? The first step in examining the proof of the resurrection is to establish the facts of the incredible claimed event historically, outside the biblical texts, but there are no credible secular firsthand historical accounts, which is an extraordinary and troubling fact. There's not one sentence from one eyewitness of the day who mentions what should have been earth-shattering breaking news and an event that would have had every historian who witnessed or had credible reporting of this supernatural event writing about it; there is not one firsthand account or passage in any historical record. Not a peep. This fact is truly troubling as it pertains to substantiating that the resurrection actually happened: humanity has no secular recording of it. No secular record. We are left with only religious or biblical texts, like those called the Gospels. The Gospels' supposed writers were named Matthew, Mark, Luke, and John. So who were Matthew, Mark, Luke, and John? They must have been extraordinary and "inspired" writers and are said to have been disciples and followers of Christ. Aside from the biblical text, is there any historical proof for the existence of even these four men, after whom the most important books of the New Testament are named? The answer is a deafening no.

Probing deeper, one discovers a larger complication regarding the Gospels, and that is that, incredibly, the four Gospels were not written by Matthew, Mark, Luke, or John! All four Gospels are hearsay writings and were originally anonymous. None claim to be written by eyewitnesses, and all were written decades later, after the crucifixion and death of the supposed son of God, Jesus Christ.

This fact brings forth a very difficult question for the Christian believer, since these "inspired" men of God, Matthew, Mark, Luke, and John, did not write the synoptic Gospels nor the book of John. Are these books still God-breathed or divinely inspired when no one has a clue as to who produced these anonymously written texts? How, then, are the four Gospels credible evidence for a resurrection when there is no historicity of the credited writers, Matthew, Mark, Luke, and John, and as far as the real writers, they are anonymous writers, not eyewitnesses, who wrote the texts decades after the claimed event? Apologists and believers may argue that there is no need to trouble oneself with who actually wrote the Gospels or whether the Gospels' authors were eyewitnesses or even received the accounts by hearsay because the Holy Spirit ensured that what they wrote was true, for whoever wrote the Gospels was working under the inspiration of the Holy Spirit.

The reasonable response here is to ask the question, If the Holy Spirit ensured that what they were writing was true, should not that same Holy Spirit have made sure that the accounts did not contradict each other as well? Yes, the Gospels contradict each other! On top of all the issues described here, the Gospels contain multiple contradictions, from who went to the tomb to who was at the tomb. It is generally accepted that, even with the best intentions, multiple individuals will not report the same event exactly the same way. We could sensibly attribute to human fallibility various minor differences in accounts that might even contradict to a slight degree, except here. We cannot and should not here, for again, we are speaking of the Bible, the supposed word of God. The Gospels would have been written under divine inspiration; the Holy Spirit was overseeing these God-breathed writings; therefore, there should be not one error or contradiction if the Gospels were truly divinely inspired.

In Matthew 28:16–17 immediately after the resurrection, the disciples go to Galilee to see Jesus. This contradicts Luke 24:33–51, where Jesus meets the disciples in Jerusalem and stays in Jerusalem until his ascension into heaven. Mark 16:5 contradicts Luke 24:4 in how many angels are at the tomb. Mark 16:5 reads, "And entering into the sepulchre, they saw a young man sitting on the right side, clothed in a long white garment; and they were affrighted." And Luke 24:4 reads, "And it came to pass, as they were much perplexed thereabout, behold, two men stood by them in shining garments." Minor variations in the same account are to be expected in our human realm but not in notable observations such as this, where one disciple reports seeing one angel and the other reports that he saw two, while both were writing these events under the inspiration of God.

Mark 16:4 reads, "And when they looked, they saw that the stone was rolled away: for it was very great." This clearly contradicts Matthew 28:2, which reads, "And, behold, there was a great earthquake: for the angel of the Lord descended from heaven, and came and rolled back the stone from the door, and sat upon it." How was it possible for Mark, while writing under the "inspiration" of God, to omit a supernatural being descending from the sky accompanied simultaneously by a great earthquake?

John 20:1–29 reads, "The first day of the week cometh Mary Magdalene early, when it was yet dark, unto the sepulchre, and seeth the stone taken away from the sepulchre." Here Mary Magdalene went to the tomb alone, yet Matthew 28:1 reads, "In the end of the sabbath, as it began to dawn toward the first day of the week, came Mary Magdalene and the other Mary to see the sepulchre." Still, Mark 16:1–2 reads, "And when the sabbath was past, Mary Magdalene, and Mary the mother of James, and Salome, had bought sweet spices, that they might come and anoint him. And very early in the morning the first day of the week, they came unto the sepulchre at the rising of the sun." We have the book of John's account stating that only one person, Mary Magdalene, went to the tomb. The book of Matthew's account states that two persons went to the tomb, they being Mary Magdalene and the other Mary, yet in the book of Mark, under the divine "inspiration" of God, the writer, whoever he may be, records three persons—Mary Magdalene, Mary the mother of James, and Salome—vising the tomb! There are a considerable number of contradictions within these four Gospels, and I do not wish to list them all here, for one contradiction renders the claim unreliable within itself.

Let's recap the proof, or lack thereof, for the claim that a man named Jesus died on a cross and rose from the dead.

1. There are no credible secular historical writings of a resurrection or of a man named Jesus returning to life after being killed on a cross in any ancient historical record.

2. The Jesus Christ crucifixion-and-resurrection story is mentioned only in religious texts.

3. There is no historicity for Matthew, Mark, Luke, or John.

4. The four Gospels were not written by Matthew, Mark, Luke, or John, and they were written decades after the Jesus Christ crucifixion-and-resurrection claim, and even if the Gospels had been written during the time of the crucifixion, there is no historicity of their existence.

5. It is a fact that to this day the writers of the four Gospels remain a mystery. No one knows who wrote the Gospels. Not knowing who wrote the Gospels weakens, if not destroys, the reliability of these writings.

6. The books named Matthew, Mark, Luke, and John contain contradicting accounts.

7. None of the Gospels are firsthand accounts of either the crucifixion or the claimed resurrection.

The proof is simply not there to support the claim that a resurrection actually happened. So what else can one do to exhaust all measures to find some proof that gives this claim a chance at possibly being true? One could make use of a conditional statement truth table here for critical thinking.

A conditional statement checks to see whether a statement is true or false. What are truth tables? *Encyclopedia Britannica* defines a truth table in logic as a "chart that shows the truth-value of one or more compound propositions for every possible combination of truth-values of the propositions making up the compound ones. It can be used to test the validity of arguments. Every proposition is assumed to be either true or false and the truth or falsity of each proposition is said to be its truth-value." [33] Basically, conditional statements are made up of two parts, a hypothesis and a conclusion, which both can be evaluated as true or false, ultimately rendering a truth value of either true or false. Here's an example: if today is Friday, then tomorrow is Sunday. The first part of the conditional statement states, "If today is Friday," which is the hypothesis. Let's pretend that today is actually

---

33 Britannica, T. Editors of Encyclopaedia. "truth table." Encyclopedia Britannica, October 15, 2022. https://www.britannica.com/topic/truth-table

Friday: we would evaluate the statement as true. Then our conclusion states, "Then tomorrow is Sunday." Here we have a contradiction, for one should know that Sunday does not come after Friday; therefore, the conclusion is evaluated as false, rendering a truth value that is also false. If both statements were false in the conditional statement, then the truth value would be true, for there would be no contradictions.

If one were to use a conditional statement truth table, how would the resurrection story fare?

In order to understand the crucifixion-and-resurrection story, one must understand why it was needed. According to the Bible, Jesus died on the cross so that humanity's sins could be forgiven; therefore, we must return to the fall-of-man story in the book of Genesis in the Garden of Eden, for this is where the cause happened and how sin entered the world through the trickery of a talking and walking snake! In the truth table, here the first statement will be the hypothesis "If the talking snake tricked humanity into eating forbidden fruit, bringing sin into the world," and the second statement, which is the conclusion, will be "then Jesus died and came back from death so that humanity's sins would be forgiven." Therefore, the conditional statement in total could be written as, "If the talking snake tricked humanity into eating forbidden fruit, bringing sin into the world, then Jesus died and came back from death so that humanity's sins would be forgiven. So, when we evaluate the first statement, what are the chances that a talking reptile tricked a human into eating fruit? In what realm is it remotely plausible that a snake was able to form thoughts and speak those thoughts to accomplish a goal outside the animal kingdom to affect humanity? It is universally known and realized that snakes do not and cannot talk. There is no scientific data suggesting that they will ever have the ability to speak. Therefore, this first statement would be viewed as invalid, or false.

Now let us examine the second statement. Is it possible for a man of flesh and blood to be killed and then, after three days of death, return back among the living? No being has ever defeated death after having been killed and buried for days. That a man purported to be the son of a deity supposedly was killed on a cross, remained dead for three days, then found his way back to his believers is an incredible story, but what is more incredible than the supposed resurrection is the factual silence of the historians of that time, for not one penned a sentence of what should have been a stop-the-presses moment for a man-was-killed-yet-he-lives-again story! How could an event of this magnitude have gone unnoticed by the historians of that time? It is unfathomable that such a spectacular event happened, a live, breathing being put to death and that same being defeating death to return among the living, and the historians simply ignored it. The only reasonable explanation for why the record keepers or historians of that time didn't make mention of such an incredible tale is that it never happened! When one considers all reasonable possibilities regarding a being returning from death after three days, one would logically consider the second statement also invalid, or false. The truth value here would be true, meaning that both statements are invalid or that it is true that both statements are false, thus rendering the resurrection story a falsehood.

If apologists and believers disagree with the truth table computations just rendered here, perhaps Christians have one more possibility of proving the claim that a man named Jesus Christ did rise from the dead, for he was the claimed Messiah. Let's go to the heart of the matter. Let's go to the people who would know the Messiah better than anyone else on earth, a source that should provide irrefutable evidence for or against Jesus Christ's resurrection story, for this source is a people whom I briefly wrote of earlier and who, as it is written in the Bible, have a covenant with God, for they are the chosen people of God, the Jews.

In the book of Deuteronomy 14:2 the holy, inspired writing reads, "For thou art an holy people unto the Lord thy God, and the Lord hath chosen thee to be a peculiar people unto himself, above all the nations that are upon the earth." Surely the chosen people of God could add some valuable context to the resurrection story to assist in validating the incredible claim of the prophesied Messiah, Jesus Christ. But again, we have a problem: not only do the modern-day Jews reject the belief that Jesus is God or the prophesied Messiah, but they also believe that a crucifixion was simply unnecessary! And more problematic still, there is a growing recognition and acceptance of the age-old claim, said to be based on historical and now DNA evidence, that the original Israelites or Jews were Black and from Africa. This produces a contentious question: If the original Jews were indeed Black and an indigenous people of Africa, how did the modern-day Jews come to be recognized as white and an indigenous people of Europe? We have two possibilities to choose from, and they are that either the biblical God changed his mind about who his favorite people are and failed to make an "inspired" update of it in the biblical text, or the modern-day recognized European Jews have pulled off the greatest identity theft in the history of humankind with the theft of an indigenous African people's birthright, thus making it their own. I denounce anti-Semitism in all its forms, and I stand with my friends in the Jewish community, yet the question must be asked: How did the original Hebrews start out as Black people in Africa yet ended up mainly being recognized throughout the world as white Europeans?

I digress. After everything already stated herein, the modern-day Jews do not recognize Jesus as the Messiah, which ultimately means they do not believe in the resurrection story! Who better to know the deity of the Jews than the Jews? And if the Jews are saying that Jesus was no more than a teacher or prophet, like Moses and Muhammad, then who are the Christians to contest it? The crucifixion story leaves one with the possibility of multiple interpretations and is filled with numerous contradictions. It is claimed to have been written by unknown, assumed holy, inspired writers.

Now, the aforementioned rejection of Jesus as the Jewish Messiah by the Jews surely drives a stake through the heart of perhaps the greatest myth of modern times, for no one should know the biblical God more intimately than the Jews, for they invented Yahweh, for it is their belief that Judaism regards Yahweh as the God of Abraham, Isaac, and Jacob and the God of the chosen people, the Israelites—that is, the Jews. These ancient writers took the liberty of penning themselves in as the chosen people of their God, and why not? For he, Yahweh, is their invention. If the ancient Chinese were the writers of the Bible, I'm sure the Chinese would have penned in that they were the chosen people of God, or if the ancient Egyptians were authors of the Bible, they, too, would have selected themselves as their god's chosen people. No nation, tribe, or group of people would create a religion and name a people foreign to them as the chosen people if they were doing the creating of those religious texts.

So why do the Jews reject Jesus as the Jewish Messiah? Actually, the list of reasons is quite lengthy; therefore, I will not list them all here.

1. The Jews' belief is that their Jewish Messiah will be not a god but a man coming into life by natural birth; therefore, Jesus did not embody the personal qualifications of the Messiah.

2. During the era of the Messiah, universal peace and recognition of God will be observed throughout the entire world. Worldwide peace did not happen during Jesus's time, and wars and conflict continue to this very day.

3. The Second Coming of the Messiah is foreign to Judaism's teachings and is viewed as a Christian invention by many, for the real Messiah will get it right on the first visit.

4. The Messiah will be a direct descendant of King David, yet Jesus is supposedly the son of Yahweh, who came into the world with the assistance of the Holy Spirit and without sexual intercourse—or, in other words, via Mary's sinless conception, known as the Immaculate Conception. This renders Jesus not a direct descendant of King David. (Note: To make matters worse, even if there were some biblical genealogies to show a link to King David, it would not be confirmable, for there is no substantial secular historical evidence that King David existed.)

5. The Messiah, as prophesied, was to return the Jews to their homeland, but when Jesus supposedly was on earth, the Jews were already living in their land.

6. The Jewish Messiah was to rebuild the temple in Jerusalem, but the temple was standing during Jesus's time on earth.

7. The Jewish Bible teaches that the Messiah would redeem Israel, but the opposite occurred after the purported crucifixion: the holy temple in Jerusalem was destroyed, and the Jews went into exile under a two-thousand-year reign of persecution.

8. The Torah teaches that the Messiah would reign as king of the Jews on earth, yet Jesus was a carpenter. Mark 6:3 reads, "Is not this the carpenter, the son of Mary, the brother of James, and Joses, and of Juda, and Simon? And are not his sisters here with us? And they were offended at him." Further, Jesus was crucified as a common criminal by the Romans and was mocked by the Romans; Mark 15:32 reads, "Let Christ the King of Israel descend now from the cross, that we may see and believe. And they that were crucified with him reviled him." Pilate's mocking inscription on the cross read, "Jesus of Nazareth, the King of the Jews," according to John 19:19–20.

9. If Jesus was the true Messiah, why did his own people, the Jews, reject him while he was on earth? And if they rejected him while he was on earth in the flesh, why are non-Jews currently surprised that the Jews reject him today?

10. The prophecies of the Messiah were to transpire during the time of the Messiah, and Jesus is quoted in the New Testament as saying that the kingdom of heaven was imminent. Matthew 3:2 reads, "And saying, Repent ye: for the kingdom of heaven is at hand." We are currently in the year 2023, and that kingdom has not come.

These are but a few examples to show just cause as to why the Jewish people reject this Jesus of the New Testament as the Jewish Messiah. When one evaluates the reasons why the Jews reject Jesus, one can reasonably understand why the Jewish people rebuff him. I listed only ten reasons, but there are a considerable number that one could add to the listed ten. The resurrection is supposedly Jesus's pinnacle act to prove to the world that he was the Messiah, yet his postresurrection appearances were limited to relatively small groups of people, and even then some of his followers within these small groups did not recognize him.

Again, there is no credible secular historical record of this spectacular tale of a man coming back from death. An act such as this would not have gone unnoticed by historians of that time. It is inconceivable to believe otherwise! To make matters worse for the believability of the resurrection story, even within the Gospels, these second- or third-hand accounts are filled with numerous contradictions and written by mystery men or anonymous writers! Then we have the purpose of the crucifixion and resurrection: these acts were done to repair that which a talking and walking snake fractured. Incredible.

Even if one does not accept the truth table illustration that I've provided that showed the crucifixion story to be invalid or false, or if one chooses not to recognize this method as credible, then I give you God's very own "chosen people," the Jews, who totally reject Jesus as their Jewish Messiah, and their evidence is overwhelming! That which has been presented in this chapter should, at a minimum, cause one to pause and reevaluate the validity of this incredible tale. The tale of a man claiming to be a god returning from the dead and attracting such a lackluster reception and a lack of recognition and historical record is simply unbelievable.

The most reasonable interpretation of the facts and points of view presented here is that the resurrection story is as likely to have occurred as the fairy tale "The Gingerbread Man," for when one earnestly considers all the facts surrounding the resurrection story of a deity named Jesus, who, it is claimed, rose from the dead, one can only reasonably conclude that the resurrection did not occur and therefore is at best a great myth.

Let's examine the event called the return of Jesus, the rapture. Now, if the resurrection never happened, the chances of a rapture actually happening are about as high as the chances of flying elephants being discovered under the sea tomorrow. The rapture teachings within the Christian community, too, are not without their own problems, much like everything else about the Christian religion. 1 Thessalonians 4:16–17 reads, "For the Lord himself shall descend from heaven with a shout, with the voice of the archangel, and with the trump of God: and the dead in Christ shall rise first: Then we which are alive and remain shall be caught up together with them in the clouds, to meet the Lord in the air: and so, shall we ever be with the Lord." Here we have the primary description of the rapture, during which believers hold that both dead and living believers will also be given glorified bodies so that they will be with Jesus for all eternity. Sounds simple enough until one comes across the several pretribulation rapture concepts or doctrines. Here is where things get really confusing. I've always held the understanding that the rapture and Second Coming were the same event, but some believers see them as two separate events. I read an essay by Alan S. Bandy, who attempts to bring clarity to these multiple beliefs regarding the rapture. He states the following:

> The most common issue centered around the Rapture has to do with the timing of it. There are four main views:
> 1. Pre-Tribulation Rapture: This view maintains the rapture occurs when Jesus comes secretly to gather the church prior a seven-year Great Tribulation that precedes the return of Christ to earth.
> 2. Mid-Tribulation Rapture: This is similar to the pre-tribulation view except that it locates the rapture after the first three-and-half years at the point when the Anti-Christ assumes power.
> 3. Pre-Wrath Rapture: This position argues that the rapture will occur toward the end of the tribulation before the

outpouring of God's wrath with the bowl judgments (Rev. 16) prior to the return of Christ.

4. Post-Tribulation: This view sees the rapture as occurring simultaneous to the return of Christ at the end of the Tribulation.

Although there are serious differences between the first three views of the rapture, they all share the same perspective that the rapture is a separate event from the second coming of Christ. [34]

This looks like a big ball of man-made confusion, for that which created the falcon would not produce a web of confusion such as this. The resurrection, rapture, and Second Coming tales clearly are man-made inventions and are not worthy of being attributed to that which brought forth the earth, the life on it, nor the celestial wonders outside it, for to do so is a profound insult when one compares the craftsmanship of each.

---

34   Alan S. Bandy, " The Rapture Question," The Gospel Coalition, January 21, 2023, https://www.thegospelcoalition.org/essay/the-rapture-question/

CHAPTER 10

The Virtuousness of Belief

For we walk by faith, not by sight.
—2 Corinthians 5:7

We are all born free
and spend a lifetime
becoming slaves
to our own
false truths.
—Atticus

Only that which is imagined requires belief in it, for all that is real in existence requires not belief in its reality, nor is it solicited. Imagine there is a god that exists in reality, whose gender is male, as the Bible claims, and he is truly the author of all creation and of this reality that is, a creation that also consists of human beings, created with the attributes of intelligence, rationality, understanding, and awareness of the real nature and laws that govern the natural norms of the world. Then this same purported biblical deity "inspires" a book through men (and not one woman), a book that contains tales that challenge and contradict that which is in accordance with reason or logic and with the real natural laws and norms of the world (i.e., reality). This biblical deity then promises that, for those that will stop thinking and believe and have faith that the incredible tales are true in spite of the insult to their reasoning and intellect, the reward will be eternal life in a heavenly utopia where one gets to worship and serve the narcissistic, all-loving biblical deity for all eternity. After all, the most commonly held belief or interpretation of biblical scriptures regarding why God created human beings, or the sole purpose for the creation of human beings, is that it was simply for God's pleasure in being glorified through praise, love, and worship. Unfortunately for those who lack the ability to set aside their capacity for intellect and reasoning and their awareness of the laws of reality, the all-loving God will dispatch the nonbelievers to hell to be eternally damned in everlasting fire.

If the aforementioned suppositions were real, they would mean that the biblical deity is doing to humanity now what he did to Adam and Eve, but with a twist. To Adam and Eve, he gave free will but not knowledge, but now humanity has free will and great knowledge and understanding of the norms of reality, but in order to win the prize of getting that one-way, all-expenses-paid trip to paradise, one must suspend all logic, reason, and awareness of natural laws. Again, if one cannot walk in faith, the Biblical all-loving God will torment them in the ever-burning lake of fire because one failed to embrace with belief that which contradicts reality and sanity. The biblical deity cannot be the cause and human beings the purpose for the creation of the world. This is lunacy to the rational, logically sound mind!

Humankind is the most intelligent living being on planet Earth, a being endowed with attributes like those of no other living creature before his arrival on the stage of life nor concurrently. Humanity's intellectual attributes are unique, and some are exclusive, like the ability to reason and understand, for we humans have large and beautifully complex brains which allow for the capacity for knowledge, or in other words, the power of knowing. Therefore, some of the qualities that separate humankind from all other animals on the planet most fundamentally are his advanced intellectual faculties, one of these faculties being humankind's ability to reason and think logically, for no other living being in the known world asks, "Why?" Humankind, the only being under the sun with this great ability to think with reason, has, for example, utilized earth's natural resources to provide himself with better living conditions and has ascended from living in caves to living in skyscrapers, such as the Burj Khalifa in Dubai and the Shanghai Tower in China. Human beings, the bipedal beings, have advanced from traveling on foot to traveling by horse and buggy to, now, embarking on space travel. Humankind now lives in the information age, and humans have limitless information available to them literally at their fingertips.

Human beings have been successful at achieving these feats only because of the naturally endowed intellectual faculties that have allowed for a greater understanding of themselves and the world around them, yet humanity, in order to appease the Christian deity, is required to stop thinking and embrace faith and belief. These requirements are extraordinarily suspicious, for humanity is naturally wired to reason, naturally endowed with curiosity, and, too, naturally programmed with the need to know, for humans have the ability to know, and—I must reiterate yet again—are the only living beings in the entire known observable universe that have the ability to ask, "Why?" If God were factually in existence and the creator of the world, he would not require faith and belief in his existence in order for humankind to realize him versus realization through actually knowing of his existence through natural phenomena after creating humanity to be knowing beings!

If there were a real god in existence performing continuous surveillance of humanity from the cosmos, and if this real god had created humankind to be reasonable, thinking beings with the capability and capacity of understanding and knowing, then this real god would not hold faith and belief as the requirements for realizing his existence as opposed to the realization of actually knowing him through the endowed senses humanity possesses. God would, instead, have humanity realize or know him the way one realizes and knows the warmth of the sun on one's skin. For how absurd is it for a god to desire belief that he exists when it would be possible to know that he exists? A god would not create man to be a creature of logic and rationality and then, through men, "inspire" an illogical and irrational religious text called the Bible and require belief in it, with the penalty of eternal damnation in a pit of fire for any being who disbelieved in it. And if this god existed outside time, space, and matter, he would not concern himself with that which is within time, space, and matter, further demanding and desiring, seemingly psychotically, humanity's love, belief, and worship of him.

If the biblical God had actually created this worldly creation, he would not be in hiding from that which he had supposedly created, God would not create this creation, then hide from the creation! God, if God were real, would not create creation and then be totally absent from it. There is not one iota of proof that God exists or that God's gender is male and not female or nonbinary, for no man has ever seen the Christian God outside the claims written in a book called the Bible, which it so happens was written by many men. If God were a real, living divine being, every human that had ever come into this reality called life would have had a realization of God's existence, and those still living today would have full comprehension and knowledge of such a great reality through natural phenomena. There would be no need for man's written texts to be God's communication to man nor for man to be his messenger. A god would deliver his message directly to each living being himself, for a god would not have need of man to prove to man that his existence was real; God's message to all humanity would not need human input! God would communicate with all humanity through natural phenomena, for in this manner man would not be able to misunderstand, misinterpret, ban or make illegal, revise, lose, add to, subtract from, or commit any other act of manipulation of his communication or "word" to humanity. This would be godlike if God were real.

Man has no need to prove to another man that the sun is real, for all individual human beings realizes the light and warmth of the sun for their individual selves. This, too, would be how God would have humanity realize him! Man writes that the biblical God's gender is male, as the genders of all the other male-dominated societies' invented gods are, but if God were truly real and desired humankind to know of this existence, that knowledge of him or of her or of it would not be the stuff of punishment and damnation for those who did not have the capacity because of rational conflicts or who lacked the desire to believe, worship, or love him, her, or it.

A god existing in reality would come to humankind naturally, akin to the oxygen that fills one's lungs naturally: no need for another man to breathe for you. God would come to each and every one like the warmth of the sunshine on one's own skin so that one could feel the warmth for oneself; again, no need for another man to tell you how the sunshine feels on your skin. This is how one would know of God's existence for one's own self in reality, through one's natural senses and intellect; thus, there would be no need for faith and belief. Learning of God's existence would not require man to seek it through the pages of man-made written books. God would not be hiding from humanity. God would be observable in reality, experienced by all humanity, along with the animal and insect kingdoms, not just humanity. The oxygen one breathes does not require love or worship of it, nor belief. The sun maintains life for all living things on earth, yet it, too, requires no love, worship, or belief in it. A real God would be like the air one breathes, and like the sun: God would not require from humanity belief in him, her, or it, for belief in a god is a man-invented concept, as is God's gender.

Think about that for a moment: the biblical God is a man—not a woman or a nonbinary individual, but a man who had a son without a woman. The patriarchal "inspired" all-male writers of the Bible had an obvious disdain for women, but if the biblical God were real, the woman would be celebrated as his greatest creation, for it is the female gender of all living beings that brings forth life into the world, which replenishes her kind! A god would not create this world and have it be so that he is unrealizable by all the inhabitants of it naturally! All living beings would be able to discern God's existence through their natural senses or, in the case of humanity, their capabilities of intellectual comprehension accompanied by those senses—sight, touch, hearing, taste, smell—all realized in a natural physical reality.

The idea of a god recruiting man to deliver his "word" to humanity is laughable when this same god is credited with creating the sun. The Christian God apparently does not need man to deliver the warmth and light of sunshine to humanity; one would think that the same God would not need man to deliver anything he wanted to communicate to humanity, and surely that communication would not be delivered by way of a manner that could be altered, edited, revised, tampered with, banned, or restricted! The word of God would be unalterable, uneditable, unrevisable, untamperable, unbannable, and unrestrictable, for the message to man from a god would be untouchable by man, and if God did decide to deliver his message to man by way of a book, then every man, woman, and child who opened this book to read it would receive the same interpretation and the same understanding, for the message of God would be impossible to misinterpret—the message of a god who had created the world perfect would be, to man, perfectly realizable through the senses. One never misinterprets the sunshine as rain; one never misinterprets the oxygen in the air as fire. And if God had made this to be so, then his word would, too, never be capable of misinterpretation. A woman in China would be able to read the Bible in China and receive the same understanding as a man in Africa, but alas, we know this is not so. This fact alone proves that the Bible is not the message of a god and is also the reason for the many sects within the Christian faith, the many different interpretations.

This claimed "word" or message, the Bible, as mentioned earlier in this book, was written and delivered after 1,500 years of so-called God-breathed inspiration. This supposed divine word contains a talking snake, a talking ass, contradictions, errors, revisions, missing or excluded books, added books, forbidden books, anonymous authors, authors with no historicity, different versions, different interpretations, magicians, sorcerers, witchcraft, good spirits, unclean spirits, evil spirits, demons, fire-breathing monsters...I could continue here, but I feel that the reader gets the point.

Human beings—well, most of humanity—are rational and logical and more times than not use good judgment in examining a claim. The numerous flaws of the Bible, compiled with its many modifications and alterations over many centuries by man, clearly demonstrate and prove that the Bible is not the "inspired" work of any god, much less one whose own existence has never been nor could ever be proved through a written claim such as the one in this book called the Bible.

From the minds of humankind sprang forth many gods, for when human beings sought to understand their existence and the circumstances of their world as it was and failed to understand it all, humans created their own truth. The unknown has given birth to the many gods of the many cultures of this world since the dawn of civilization. The only place where God is real is in one's own mind when one believes, but once one awakens from this fantasy and the eyes become open, all gods vanish, for gods are real only within the minds and imaginations of the believers. The butterfly is not required to have faith in this biblical God, but if the biblical God created all living things, should not the animal and insect kingdoms also be required to love, believe in, and worship the biblical God too? If the biblical God were real, this God would require all living things, including the butterfly, to have faith in him. Humankind has gods because humans have the ability to create them with their great imaginations, and these creators knew that neither they nor anyone else in reality had ever experienced or seen the very gods that they themselves had created, so they had to fix this flaw and then drew on faith and belief as the tools one must possess in order to experience God. And what a magnificent strategy!

Man writes in Hebrews 11:6, "But without faith it is impossible to please him: for he that cometh to God must believe that he is, and that he is a rewarder of them that diligently seek him." What is so virtuous about believing in a talking-snake tale that supposedly caused the downfall of humanity when no human has ever seen a snake talk? There is nothing virtuous about believing in a talking snake when in reality, and outside the biblical texts, snakes do not and cannot talk! What is so virtuous about believing in Balaam's talking ass when no sane man or woman has ever witnessed a talking ass?

There are some of you who could put up a challenging argument against my last question, but I digress. There is nothing virtuous about believing that a man named Balaam had an ass that talked. A god would not create snakes and donkeys without the ability to talk in this reality, in this existence, have this limitation be known by humanity, make these animals talk for the "inspired" publication of a book, the Bible, and then desire one to believe in this fabrication, for it is utter nonsense to believe it so!

The biblical text states that the Christian God had a chosen people when he supposedly created all humanity. The sun doesn't have a chosen people; it shines on all people. The oxygen doesn't have a chosen people, for it fills the lungs of all living creatures, and if God were real, he, she, or it would not have a chosen people!

In life, if the existence of something is not a natural phenomenon but is produced by man, it then is not divine or the work of a deity or of a god; it is the work of man. What better proof of this than Joseph Smith, the American "prophet" and founder of the Church of Jesus Christ of Latter-day Saints (the Mormon church)? Many believed that Joseph Smith was a prophet of God and followed him despite the fact that his teachings harbored sexist, homophobic, and racist practices, very much like the original Christian Bible. In 1823 Joseph Smith said he was visited by an angel named Moroni. In 1830 Joseph Smith started the Mormon church, and today there are over sixteen million followers, or Mormons, worldwide! Not bad for a teaching that started in the 1800s, but that's how easy it is for a man to start a new religion or religious sect!

Outside of the fact that at least Joseph Smith was a real person, we also have Moses of the Old Testament, who literally has no historicity, but both were simply men, real or invented persons, claiming to be or purported to be prophets of God. Whether they were self-proclaimed or others believed these men to be "prophets" and proclaimed them to be so, they were just men. Again, Joseph Smith's claim is that he was visited by an angel named Moroni, and people believed him! Anyone, including me, could make that claim and start telling people—in a convincing manner, of course. For example, I could make the claim that I was visited by an angel named Thema and that I was a prophet, for I had received revelations from Jesus Christ that he didn't provide to Joseph Smith, and with that I could claim another testament of Jesus Christ or, in essence, form another religious sect and have followers and believers as well.

A god, a creator of all things, would never, in order for humanity to realize his existence, require that being that he created rational and logical, with the greatest intellectual gift in the world, the reasonable and logical mind, to close that very mind and rely on faith and belief in words written by men no greater nor lesser than that being—that is, require humanity to have faith in that holy book under the written claim by man that a god inspired it. This is utter idiocy. There is nothing virtuous about blind faith or belief when that being called humankind is naturally designed rational and logical, with the ability to understand, perceive, discern, and realize—with the exclusive gift denied all other living beings, the ability or power to know. Belief or faith is needed only when one entertains myths, legends, fairy tales, or any of the many genres of falsehoods, but that which is real and factual does not need belief; it is not subject to opinion based on belief or faith or what one thinks, feels, or hopes is real but is rather based on reality and that which can be proved. The ability to believe in a God that supposedly punished all unborn humanity because a talking snake tricked a woman into eating fruit God had deemed forbidden is not a demonstration of high moral excellence or, even remotely, virtue.

What this belief does demonstrate is that humanity is still ignorant and afraid, for religion is the shadow of ignorance and fear. If God were a reality, one would not be required to close one's mind to realize him. This is akin to a god requiring the eagle to slither on the soil of the earth like the snake in order to realize him, when it is designed for flight, or requiring the snake, which is not designed for flight, to take flight like the eagle in order to realize his existence. This would be unreasonable—just as unreasonable as it would be for a real God to ask the human being to become unnatural by requiring humanity to cease doing that which no other living being is capable of, thinking rationally and logically.

The Bible states that the Christian God requires one's belief, not that rational- and logical-thinking stuff. Hebrews 11:6 reads, "But without faith it is impossible to please him: for he that cometh to God must believe that he is, and that he is a rewarder of them that diligently seek him." Rationality and logic cause too many problems, for if one were allowed to think as a Christian, then one, for example, would perhaps take issue with God creating the woman Eve and the man Adam ignorant of good and evil in the "Fall of Man" story, in which they were not capable of knowing good from evil, even though the Christian God made the snake intelligent, with the ability to saunter and talk. "Now the serpent was more subtil than any beast of the field which the Lord God had made": thus reads Genesis 3:1 The snake was created more clever or intelligent than Adam and Eve, yet they were created to keep sin out of the world against the more intelligent reptile or against Lucifer, one of the most powerful of all created angels, depending on which narrative one embraces.

Regardless, a real God would not have set up humanity with two people to keep sin out of the world when they were not capable of succeeding. The Christian believer would have to ask rational questions, such as, Why would God intervene by stopping Balaam from putting a curse on the Israelites in Moab and take the liberty of making it possible for Balaam's ass to talk so as to inquire why Balaam was beating him in the process, yet the same God stood silent as Nazi Germany under Adolf Hitler murdered approximately six million European Jews? The same God of the Bible stood silent for almost four hundred years as Africans were shipped like cattle during the transatlantic slave trade, also known as the Euro-American slave trade, during which over ten million Africans arrived in the Americas while some two million perished en route. These Africans were subjected to murder, rape, mental and physical torture and abuse, and forced labor, and the effects of that savagery are visible today in America in 2023, yet the biblical God stopped not one slave ship en route to America. One can only imagine the suffering, torment, cries, and prayers just to be free, but no God delivered the Black African slaves out of their bondage, out of this hell. Frederick Douglass, born enslaved, was quoted as saying, "I prayed for twenty years but received no answer until I prayed with my legs."

Today the Catholic church is seemingly a haven for pedophiles, and according to some reports, the problem is centuries old. The vast majority of these sexual-predator priests of the Catholic church escape punishment by local and state law enforcement agencies, as well as from the now very quiet God of the Bible. But to his credit, the biblical God stopped Balaam from putting a *curse* on the Israelites and made sure Balaam got the message by making his ass talk.

Humans, beings naturally wired for logical and rational thinking, would receive any message meant for them from the creator of them and of the world through natural phenomena, not through the intermediary of a man-made, man-written book called the Bible. Any message from a god would be in harmony with humankind's ability to comprehend it, naturally. God's message would not need one man to explain to another man or woman what God is saying by giving interpretations from this man-written book known as the Bible. God, if he were an actual reality, would not create humanity as reasonable and logical, then deliver an illogical and unreasonable message to humanity, through humanity, in written texts requiring humanity not to be analytical but to have belief and faith in it. A god would not ask humankind to walk by faith and not by sight when humankind is created as the greatest thinking, analytical being in the known creation! As mentioned previously, a god would not ask for flight from the snake or slithering from the eagle; so, too, would a god not ask the most intelligent, thinking being in the universe to cease thinking to realize him. There is nothing virtuous, especially morally, in a being that is designed to think, then chooses not to because a book written by men states that he should. This requires the reasonable man to now become unreasonable, and this requirement would never come from that which brought forth the creation.

The Bible cannot be the divine word of that which brought forth creation. The Bible, along with all other man-written texts, is not a revelation from that which created the world but is the word of man, for a god such as the one described in the Bible does not exist. The truth is as clear as day as far as who or what created what or whom; that which brought forth creation and all its natural phenomena is the cause of the world, and anything that has human input is human invention.

Through fear and ignorance, one discovers gods, but through analytical thinking, study, and research, one discovers understanding; one discovers the truth. Through reasoning and logical thinking, primarily in the field of science, humanity has made extraordinary discoveries using the mind. This is a fact. Now, then, why would a god require humanity to now not think and just believe? I say this is not the requirement of a supernatural-phenomenon God but that of a man-made god. Modern-day gods are no more real than the dead ancient gods of yesterday. When the sands of time bring an end to civilizations, the believers of their gods die, and so, too, die the gods that were believed in by those civilizations.

Creation did not bring forth gods, for gods did not exist before the arrival of humans. From the minds of men, gods sprang forth, cloaked with emotions and traits similar to those of the very men who created them. Only the beings called humans yearn for veneration, worship, and love and, too, desire from others belief and faith in them. No other being in existence possesses these needs, only the human being—and the many gods created by the beings called humans.

It should be no wonder why the biblical God desires worship, love, and belief in him, for the men who created the Christian God created this deity in their image, assigning their attributes to this God. There is nothing fundamentally unique about the God of the Bible. It could be argued that Christianity is nothing more than an evolved religion that plagiarized or adapted concepts from religions that pre-dated Christianity by thousands of years, from perhaps the oldest religion, the Kemetic (Egyptian) spirituality. Because Kemet (modern-day Egypt) was an African society, prejudice and bias cloud the debate, and the attempt is to not recognize this religion as the oldest because it's an indigenous African religious spirituality, but I digress. Other ancient religions that gave Christianity some of its basic tenets also are Mithraism, Zoroastrianism, and Hinduism. Further still, Christianity, along with Islam, is simply a revised edition of Judaism. There is nothing exceptional about the religion called Christianity; again, it is a spin-off of Judaism.

So then, why should one believe that the religion called Christianity is the only real inspired word or message from God that is true, and all the other thousands of religions, ancient and new, are false? It is difficult at best to believe that a real deity exists when literally thousands of religions and millions of gods within those religions have been presented to the world since man embarked upon the god-creating business. The many religions demonstrate that "God" is a man-made concept. From the oldest religions of ancient times out of Africa (Kemetic) to those of the modern era, man has long been conjuring up deities and religions! Since the dawn of civilization, man has created his gods in his image, for apparently deity creation is not very difficult: create them, and man will come, for humanity wants to believe, for what the heart wants, the mind creates. From ancient Africa's creators of deities to Joseph Smith to L. Ron Hubbard, man has long been in the deity-making business.

Lafayette Ronald Hubbard was primarily a novelist, or a writer of books of fiction and fantasy, who, in the 1950s, founded the Church of Scientology, which has been one of the most successful new religions to emerge in the past century. Imagine a man who was a writer of fiction creating a religion. Who would have thought? Like Lafayette Ronald Hubbard's Scientology, all religions were started by men, their texts penned by men, and their deities created by men. The biblical text 2 Corinthians 5:7, which states, "For we walk by faith, not by sight," was written in a book by man under the supposed "divine inspiration" from God, and believers are required to have faith that these writings were indeed communicated to the writers from God.

What is so morally virtuous about having faith and belief in a purported invisible deity and religious texts literally incomprehensible to the reasonable mind that the Christian God would desire these above all other traits of moral virtues or qualities of ethical righteousness when belief and faith in the unbelievable are not characteristics of good moral character and are not measurements of a person's level of morality or ethics? Psychology speaks of virtues such as wisdom and knowledge, courage, humanity, justice, temperance, and transcendence. If the deity of the Christian faith were a real divine being that had created all species of snakes without the ability to talk, what are the chances that he (God) would make just one talk, according to the "inspired" Bible, then require humanity to have belief and faith in the fall-of-man story, thus holding up the capability of believing that a talking snake seduced a female human being into eating forbidden fruit as a higher moral virtue than the aforementioned virtuous traits of wisdom and knowledge, courage, humanity, justice, temperance, and transcendence?

Aristotle defined moral virtue, along with intellectual virtues, as "exemplified by courage, temperance, and liberality; the key intellectual virtues are wisdom, which governs ethical behaviour, and understanding, which is expressed in scientific endeavour and contemplation." Man wrote, in the biblical texts, "walk by faith and not by sight" for a reason, for to embrace the Christian faith, one must stop thinking in order for there not to be reasonable mental conflicts. For example, one is to believe that the Christian God placed two ignorant people in a garden, innocent as lambs, to be the guardians and protectors for keeping sin and evil out of the world where sin and evil supposedly didn't exist, and incredibly, I must reiterate that, by design, this God of the Bible made Adam and Eve ignorant of good and evil, but lo and behold, the biblical God made the snake the most intelligent creature in the garden. Remember that Genesis 3:1 reads, "Now the serpent was more subtil than any beast of the field which the Lord God had made." Ask yourself, Why would a god create two people ignorant of evil, place the tree of knowledge of good and evil in the middle of the Garden of Eden, then make the snake the wisest of all the animals in the garden while the fate of all humanity lay in the balance? The reasonable mind would conclude that the Christian God either wasn't serious about keeping sin out of the world or was simply an incompetent deity—or maybe still, the fall-of-man story never happened, and the God of the Bible, like all the other numerous deities that humankind once believed in and those deities that believers still regard as real, is also a falsehood. Nature was wise not to create gods; therefore, none exist. Man is the only being on earth intelligent enough to create gods and the only being on earth with the ignorance to believe in them. All species of animals and insects are beings that are at peace with their existence except for humanity, due to humanity's natural intelligence and unquenchable hunger, the need to know and understand—for in the infancy of humanity's attempt to understand the world and itself, it stands to reason that where human beings could not find understanding, human beings created gods.

The fact that man wrote the Bible is all the proof needed that man created the god within its written pages. The Bible's claims are written by men who wrote that God communicated to them these inspired writings in this man-written book called the Bible. The writings are those of man, and so are their claims; so, too, is the physical manufacturing of the book: all created by man; nothing divine to witness here. It's simple, actually, for it is what it is. If a New York City rat were born in a castle, this wouldn't make it a prince; it's still a New York City rat. If a lion cub were born in an American hospital nursery ward, this wouldn't make it a cute toddler; it would still be a carnivorous predator. And an incredible, unproved religious claim written and propagated by society's most highly honored and respected men doesn't make that claim an empirical truth: it is still an incredible, unproved religious claim.

As mentioned earlier in this writing, that which brought forth the world requires not love, belief, or worship from humanity; only man requires these confirmations. And if there were a god needing these acts from humanity, he, she, or it would not need human input in communicating this need to humanity. For example, the next time a Jehovah's Witness knocks on your door, waking you up at 7:00 a.m. on a Saturday morning proclaiming that the purpose of this visit to your home is to bring you the word of God after you've worked a sixty-hour week, kindly and respectfully ask, Why does Jehovah have need of your services? He supposedly delivers to humanity the sunshine yet requires assistance when delivering his word? And would not the word of God be akin to the light of the sun, for how is it that you can carry the word of God in a book that can fit in your pocket yet cannot carry the light and warmth of the sun in a book and place that in your pocket?

I now digress and ask again, still, How is it that we be? We (humanity) at this time in human history simply do not know, but one thing I am confident in is that a god such as the biblical deity did not create man, for man created the biblical deity as man created the gods before Jehovah and after Jehovah; sound reasoning instructs me to conclude this; further, as stated previously, if there were a god, humanity would come know of him, her, or it without mankind's input. Just as humanity realizes the warmth and light of the sun through natural phenomena, so, too, would humanity realize a god in the same manner. There would be no need for belief. A god or creator of the world would not create humankind with a mind capable of reason, then make the realization of his existence unreasonable to that mind, then, too, requiring belief in it. God would not need humanity to turn off the mind to realize his existence or make the request of humanity to walk by faith and not by sight; this is the work of man, not that of a divine deity, for in the man-written book the Bible, 2 Corinthians 5:7, a verse accredited to a man named Paul, says, "We walk by faith, not by sight." A god would not need a created being to become less in creation than what he, she, or it is in order to realize his, her, or its (God's) existence.

If a god such as the one in the Christian Bible truly existed, humanity would not need to believe that God is true. Humanity would know that God is true. God would not subject humanity to belief in writings penned by man that contradict reality and secular facts and that are also saturated with confusing, mystifying jargon, dual meanings, and literally or metaphorically rambling riddles. A god or the creator would not indulge in this hocus-pocusing of humanity. The Bible is not the word of God; it is the word of man, for God's sake (no pun intended).

Man, not a supernatural being, deity, or God, wrote the Bible; and with all due respect to those of you who earnestly seek something greater to believe in outside of yourself to better tolerate a cruel and at times seemingly hopeless world, my goal is not to take away from you that which you love and believe is real, for I wish I could give unto humanity something with more bells and whistles, yet I have only the truth. Be not one who needs a placebo to find purpose in life, for it is better to understand and to know than to close one's eyes and fantasize a truth.

Let's acknowledge a few realities. It is a fact that *Homo sapiens* (Adam and Eve) were not the first humans on earth but that we are the last remaining humans. One can accept the factual, provable scientific evidence regarding this, or one can choose to believe in the Adam and Eve story with the talking snake. We know that the story of Noah and the ark is not a historical fact simply because of the civilizations that were flourishing during the approximate time period of this supposed biblical flood and that had no disruption in their historical timeline of existence—great civilizations such as Egypt, Mesopotamia, China's Neolithic dynasty, and many others! One can choose to believe the historical record or choose to believe that a six-hundred-year-old man named Noah was warned by the biblical God that he was upset with humanity and that he was going to kill everything on earth by flooding the planet for forty days and forty nights, of which there is no evidence or secular recorded history.

The Bible was penned by men who were in their infancy in terms of understanding themselves and the world. For example, if mortality or death did not exist in all creation, those writers would have invented a story to accommodate this reality and might have written something such as the following:

> And it came to pass when the crafty serpent saw the woman admiring the forbidden fruit on the tree of knowledge of good and evil, the serpent walked over to the woman and began to beguile the woman. The serpent, being cleverer than any of God's creations he had made, said to the woman, "Did God really say, 'You must not eat fruit from any tree in the garden'?"
>
> The woman said to the serpent, "We may eat fruit from the trees in the garden. But God did say, 'You must not eat the fruit from the tree of knowledge of good and evil. We are not permitted to even touch it. If you do, you will die.'"
>
> "You will certainly not die," the serpent said to the woman. "God knows that when you eat fruit from that tree, you will know things you have never known before. Like God, you will be able to tell the difference between good and evil." As the woman stretched out her hand to grasp the forbidden fruit, the man, Adam, appeared and pushed away the hand of

Eve and chased the serpent away, thus saving the world from sin and death.

Later, in the cool of the evening, God came through the garden yelling, "Adam, where are you?" and found Adam sitting with the woman. God, sensing the anger in Adam, asked, "Adam, why are you not happy?"

Adam said, "The woman that you made for me almost brought death and sin into the world, but I stopped her from eating the forbidden fruit."

God turned to the woman. "Is this true, woman?"

Eve confessed, "Yes, the serpent beguiled me, but the man, Adam, prevented me from bringing sin and death into the world by pushing my hand away. But Lord, what if the serpent tries again and I am alone without the man, Adam? I may fail."

God, after hearing this, became angry and turned to Adam. "Adam, since you obeyed me and saved the world from sin and death, you shall rule over all beasts in the garden and the woman." God then turned to Eve and said, "Since you would have disobeyed me if not for the man, Adam, stopping you, from this day forth, the man shall rule over you, and you shall bear his children. Childbirth's pain shall be your punishment and the punishment of all women."

When God was done with the woman, God went looking for the serpent, and once God found it, God stomped the ground in anger and said to the serpent, "From this day forth, ye shall never walk upright again, so on your belly you go!" And when the snake attempted to plead for mercy, God said, "And from this day forward you will never speak another word again!" Then God said, "Today was a good day."

If the biblical God were indeed the designer of life, and being all-knowing, all-powerful and all-loving, he would not have made the serpent the smartest creature in the Garden of Eden; God would have made Adam and Eve the smartest, and even if they had not been the wisest, God would have at least made them with the ability to distinguish between good and evil! Christians and apologists will argue that God, in the book of Genesis's fall-of-man story, was testing humanity to make sure that humanity loved him. This is why God designed the conditions that he did. This is absurd to the reasonable mind; this test of love and obedience is comparable to a god testing a fish that he created with only the ability to swim, telling it to now climb a tree to demonstrate its love and obedience to him.

The Bible cannot be the inspired work of that which brought forth creation, for it insults one's reason and intellect; that which brought forth the creation, if it were to have a message for humanity, would communicate it to humanity in a natural, harmonious manner that would not insult one's natural, reasonable mind. Fact: the Bible was written by man. Fact: that the Bible was written under the "inspiration" of a god is the claim that, too, was written into the Bible by man. There is nothing divine about those two facts that should persuade one to logically conclude that a supernatural being must in some ways have orchestrated its writings and now holds that one is morally obligated to believe the claims within it.

Previously in this writing, I respectfully asked, What is so spectacular about this man-written book called the Bible, and what separates it from all other religious writings? The answer is that there simply is nothing there. One need not look further for evidence of the frailty and puniness of this man-made religious text called the Bible than the "Jefferson Bible," edited to the liking of Thomas Jefferson himself, for example. Yes, Jefferson, a man who had hundreds of Black African slaves and even had a fourteen-year-old slave girl as his sexual property; she even bore him as many as six children. By today's standards, he would be regarded as a rapist and pedophile. Human reason begs to ask, How would it be possible for a slave owner and rapist to change or edit the word of God? Man cannot edit or change the wings of a common house fly, yet the "inspired" word of God can be altered so easily and by the likes of men such as Jefferson!

And the most startling aspect of this one alteration of the "divine" word this time or the many other times before Jefferson's alterations is that the biblical God did not toss a thunderbolt or send an angel or do anything to stop Jefferson from altering his "inspired" and sacred word to humanity. Why did the biblical God do nothing? In order for one to embrace the Bible as the divine word of a god, one would have to walk by faith—that is, trust and believe—and not by sight. That is, one must shut down one's mind, for if one were to keep the light of reason activated in the mind, one would have no option but to reject Christianity. Any oral or written request to have one stop thinking and simply have faith and belief in an unproven claim without evidence is not the work of a divine being; the only being in existence that can make this request is another human being. For no other being in existence can verbally communicate this or provide a written request asking humanity not to think but to believe that the Bible is a message from the creator of the world and not from man.

In this time, the original manuscripts of God's "inspired" word, the light of the world, have been lost. No original "inspired" manuscripts of the Bible or God's message to humanity exist, yet the original sun still sits in the sky. The Bible is claimed to be the light of the world, the living word of this God, but the original has been lost. If it be true that the biblical God created the sun and "God-breathed" the Bible, then just like the sun, his original word would never have become lost. An all-knowing God would have perhaps made plans for a mishap like the loss of his word, or better yet, would have every newborn child come out of the womb with his or her own original copy!

Finally, the Bible would have one believe that walking by faith and not by sight makes one morally exceptional and virtuous in the sight of the biblical God. Imagine that: not thinking pleases that which created humankind to think and to think far more greatly than any being that ever lived; this creator now desires one to not think, not reason, not make sense of, just have faith, and the biblical God will reward the one who is created rational for believing in that which is utterly irrational.

Yes, from the beginning of time, man has asked the age-old question, How is it that we be? And in the infancy of humankind's journey toward understanding that which humanity could not understand or make sense of, humankind simply filled in the blanks by creating gods. Over time and up to today, through scientific discovery and research, many gods were sent into retirement, for humankind now has knowledge of and understands what causes the thunder and lighting, the rain, and the rising and setting of the sun, to list but a very few examples. Humanity is no longer in the infancy of its understanding of itself and of the world; the art of hocus-pocusing the masses using fear and ignorance is over. Humankind now knows that Earth is not at the center of the universe and that the sun does not revolve around it. Humankind now knows that the universe is more than six thousand years old and that Adam and Eve could not have possibly been the first humans on planet Earth. Humankind now knows that a talking snake never played a role in bringing death into creation.

Walking by sight and not by faith is not the request of that which brought forth this reality, this world, and humanity. This request came from humankind; this request came from man. Outside the believer's mind, God, the devil, hell, and heaven cannot be found, but inside the mind of the believer, anything is possible, even the talking snake. Many who believe in the biblical God care not about scientific facts and reason and are fierce defenders of the faith even in the face of these. The faith gives them permission to deny that which is objectively true. Snakes do not talk, be they possessed by an evil agent or not, and humankind is endowed with reason: these are objective truths. The biblical God, if he were truly a divine being existing in reality, creating a world along these norms that corresponded with reality, would not give humankind understanding of the actuality of this reality but then require humanity to believe in that which conflicts with that understanding and reality, thus deeming this belief virtuousness; furthermore, punishment from this all-loving God of the Bible with eternal damnation in a lake of fire for the disbelief in it would be severely demented.

The very foundation of the Christian faith is predicated on belief in the Adam and Eve tale with the talking snake. That which brought forth this reality would not create snakes without the ability of human speech, then require one to believe that one snake did have a conversation with a human of the female gender through an "inspired" book written by man. If the God of the Bible were real, God, then, would not be a subjective truth; God would be an objective fact. Christianity, at best, like all other religions that preceded it, was humankind's best, although flawed, effort to explain the origins of the existence of life and of the world as humans understood it to be during those ancient times, but at worst, Christianity and all those religions that preceded it and those that came after it are perhaps the greatest psychological tricks or hoaxes or exploitations ever devised by religious jugglers for their pleasure, wealth, and, of course, power.

I must reiterate—and feel that it cannot be overstated—that one could reason thus: if the creator of this world desired to communicate with humanity, it would be through the voice of nature, not a penned work that is man's interpretation of a claimed inspiration. Further, it can also be presumed that any penned work by man claiming to be the work of that which brought forth creation is a counterfeit, for any book written by man is beneath the craftmanship of that which placed the sun in the sky and created the caterpillar with the ability to transform into the butterfly.

When one chooses to walk by faith and not by sight in the religious sense, then one lives in the mental realm of religious faith and belief and not the realm of reality. This incredible existence called life exists not in the realm of fantasy but in that realm of actuality and reality and therefore was not brought forth by something or someone outside reality or by any other man-invented religious hocus-pocus.

Author Biography

James Z. Cox is a former Marine who is currently employed as an Information Technology Specialist (Network and VoIP) at a military hospital. James graduated valedictorian of his class earning an Associate of Science degree in Information Technology in 2006 and in 2008 graduated as the valedictorian of his class earning a Bachelor of Science degree in Information Systems Security from ITT Technical Institute-San Bernardino, California. His hobbies are working out (weight training) and reading (closet nerd). Ever curious and philosophical, James is constantly researching information for greater knowledge and understanding of the reality of being and enjoys intellectually stimulating conversations or debates. His writing is inspired by his insatiable need to question and to make sense of that which much of the world unnecessarily fears. James currently resides in California.